MY LIFE

Sport Media S
A Trinity Mirror Business

MY LIFE

Copyright © Kenny Dalglish

SportMedia
A Trinity Mirror Business

Published by Trinity Mirror Sport Media
Managing Director: Ken Rogers
Senior Editor: Steve Hanrahan
Editor: Paul Dove
Senior Art Editor: Rick Cooke

Senior Sub-editor: Roy Gilfoyle
Sub-editor: Chris McLoughlin
Design: Colin Sumpter, Alison Barkley
Senior Marketing Executive: Claire Brown
Senior Book Sales Executive: Karen Cadman

Interviews by: Ken Rogers

First Edition
Published in hardback in Great Britain in 2013.
Published and produced by: Trinity Mirror Sport Media,
PO Box 48, Old Hall Street, Liverpool L69 3EB.

ISBN: 9781908695550

Photography: Tony Woolliscroft, Trinity Mirror, Liverpool Post & Echo,
the Kenny Dalglish collection, PA Images

Printed and bound in the UK by CPI Colour

Dedication

To my own family and a special football family

It all starts with your mum and dad. They sacrifice everything for you to enjoy football and have the opportunity to become a professional footballer.

I'll aways be grateful to my mum, Cathy, and dad, Bill, for that, and my big sister Carol.

Where I was brought up and how I was brought up has shaped me and it has been the same for my wife Marina. Both sets of parents had similar principles and I hope we've continued in the same way.

You need a good family life. It allows you to go to work knowing everything's good. I couldn't have achieved what I have without the support from Marina and my family. They are the ones that get the upheaval but they have always supported me in what I wanted to do in football.

Our four children have been a fantastic credit to their mother. When they were growing up I was playing football. You spend as much time with them as you can

and do your best but they have been formed by their mother.

Kelly and Paul may have been more high profile through their jobs but Lynsey and Lauren are a credit to the family as well. They are maybe a wee bit under the radar but we are equally proud of them all.

I suppose the common denominator in my personal life and football life is a family ethos.

The football clubs I played for were exactly the same. Appreciative of everything the supporters did for them and so humble. They never took any of that for granted.

I've been a very lucky boy. To play for two of the most successful clubs of that time in British football is fantastic.

I owe so much to everyone at Celtic Football Club and to the supporters who were really encouraging.

When it comes to my gratitude and appreciation for the supporters at Liverpool Football Club, I don't think I'll ever be able to show them how much me and my family appreciate everything that they have done for us.

CONTENTS

PAISLEY'S TRIBUTE TO 'KING' KENNY

'He's unique, he thinks soccer 24 hours a day'

By GRAHAM CLARK

I've enjoyed going back to my roots for this book

It's hard to believe that 45 years have passed since I signed professional terms with Celtic Football Club at the age of 17. It was all football, football, football for me as a wee boy, but I could never have imagined how my life in the game would have panned out.

I went from playing in goal for my school team to representing two of the biggest football clubs in the world and appearing for my country over 100 times. I'll never take playing for Celtic, Liverpool or Scotland for granted – it was a privilege to have done so.

Memories of my childhood in Glasgow came flooding back to me when I put this book together.

I travelled back to my home city and visited the home where I grew up on Mingulay Street, my old primary school and both Celtic Park and Hampden Park.

It reminded me how fortunate I was to have a supportive family, teachers and coaches who would give up their spare time on evenings and weekends so bairns like me could play football. Such support should never be underestimated by anyone in the game.

I also returned to Anfield to spend time in the Kop museum where many of the medals and awards I won as a player and manager at Liverpool Football Club are on display.

Sharing photos of those medals, trophies and the stories behind them in my book is a way in which I can say thanks for all the incredible support I've received from Celtic and Liverpool fans over the years.

I enjoyed my time at Blackburn too. To win the Premier League trophy was very special and I've not forgotten my spell with Newcastle, or my team-mates, managers and players.

Both Liverpool and Celtic have supporters all over the world who may not be able to visit Merseyside or Glasgow to see some of the things we won as a team.

I hope this book gives you all the opportunity to do that and revives your own memories of some of the great nights I was fortunate to experience during my career.

WHERE IT ALL STARTED

My education in life, and in football,
began in my Glasgow home

Me with my sister Carol and my mum and dad

Heroes in my home and on the pitch

My first heroes were my mother and father, Cathy and Bill – then the football side kicked in!

I was born in the east end of Glasgow on March 4, 1951. Then we moved to the north end. You didn't have too many heroes apart from your mother who was feeding you. We stayed there until I was about 14 years old and then moved down to the south side, right next to Ibrox.

My dad was a Rangers supporter. As a kid you normally support the team your dad supports because he takes you to the matches, so I grew up in my school years as a Rangers fan.

We had Rangers, Celtic, Queens Park, Clyde, and Partick Thistle, all in Glasgow with a population of a million people in those days. It was difficult to avoid a football stadium and even more difficult to avoid taking an interest in football, especially as my dad was always into it.

He was a good amateur player in his day. He went to the match with his dad and his workmates. In an industrial city like Glasgow it's difficult to avoid football.

About Glasgow:

Glasgow (*Scots: Glesca; Scottish Gaelic: Glaschu*) *is the largest city in Scotland. It is situated on the River Clyde in the country's West Central Lowlands. Inhabitants of the city are referred to as Glaswegians.*

Glasgow grew from a small rural settlement on the River Clyde to become one of the largest seaports in the world. Expanding from the medieval bishopric and royal burgh, and the later establishment of the University of Glasgow in the 15th century, it became a major centre of the Scottish Enlightenment in the 18th century. From the 18th century the city also grew as one of Great Britain's main hubs of transatlantic trade with North America and the West Indies.

Glasgow was known as the "Second City of the British Empire" for much of the Victorian era and Edwardian period. Today it is one of Europe's top ten financial centres and is home to many of Scotland's leading businesses.

In the late 19th and early 20th centuries Glasgow grew in population, eventually reaching a peak of 1,128,473 in 1939.

In the 1960s, comprehensive urban renewal projects resulting in large-scale relocation of people to new towns and peripheral suburbs, followed by successive boundary changes, have reduced the current population of the City of Glasgow council area to 592,000, with 1,199,629 people living in the Greater Glasgow urban area. The entire region surrounding the conurbation covers approximately 2.3 million people, 41% of Scotland's population.

The world's first international football match was held in 1872 at the West of Scotland Cricket Club's Hamilton Crescent ground in the Partick area of the city. The match, between Scotland and England, finished 0–0.

Hampden Park, which is Scotland's national football stadium, holds the European record for attendance at a football match: 149,547 saw Scotland beat England 3-1 in 1937.

Famous Glaswegians include poet Robert Burns, explorer David Livingstone, Sir Alexander Fleming, who discovered penicillin, singer Lulu and comedian Billy Connolly.

A Google map that shows that if you grew up in Glasgow, you were surrounded by football!

Year Of The Rabbit
March 4, 1951

On the Chinese calendar the year of the rabbit represents hope. People born under the sign of the rabbit are said to be gentle, sensitive, compassionate, amiable, modest and merciful, and have strong memory. They like to communicate with others in a humorous manner. They are softly-spoken and welcoming.

Me in my
street
football
days

Playing for Madrid...but not for Real

In those days you were not too bothered about wearing Celtic or Rangers jerseys to show your support. There were no replica kits as such. There wasn't the market there is now.

I think the only other strip I can remember kids having back then was a red strip with white sleeves. It was probably Arsenal. There was not a lot to choose from!

When I was seven or eight we had a street team that we called Milton Madrid. I don't know how we ended up all wearing the same maroon strip. We probably got them for Christmas.

We called ourselves Milton Madrid because the same letter started both words. It wasn't because we were Madrid fans. In those days, like now, Real Madrid was a fantastic club and everyone

remembers them beating Eintracht Frankfurt at Hampden in the European Cup Final in 1960.

I was nine at the time and at half-time in that game we were out in the street having our own match which was more important to us than the European Cup Final itself.

Then we went back in and watched the second half of the game on the telly.

We played with a Frido plastic ball, or maybe a Wembley. It certainly wouldn't have been an expensive one.

At school, someone would bring out a ball made of thick plastic called a Mould Master which many of the schools used. It was more like a basketball and very difficult to burst. We could never afford one of them to play with in the street...unless somebody pinched one from the school!

WITH THE COMPLIMENTS OF **Ty·Phoo** Tea LTD., BIRMINGHAM 5

GRAHAM WILLIA
(West Bromwich Albion an
Graham Williams played for Rhyl as a schoolboy before joini
league debut against Blackpool later in the same year. Gra
against Ireland in the 1959/60 season. Two of his achievem
the F.A. Cup and the League Cup against Everton and We

WITH THE COMPLIMENTS OF **Ty·Phoo** Tea LTD., BIRMINGHAM 5

Ron D
to No
and in
joint t

ROGER HUNT (Liverpool)

HAYNES (Fulham)

Card marked

I was more of a collector of football
cards than stickers. You would buy the
chewing gum and collect the cards.
I think we used to get them in cereal
packets as well.

Before going to the match we used
to have a special newspaper previewing
the big game of the day which had
black and white pictures of the players
as well, so there was always something
for us to collect as kids.

My bedroom

I shared a bedroom with my elder sister Carol. I might have stuck up pictures that you got in the souvenir newspapers before the matches, but there weren't a great deal of photographs on the wall.

And there was no central heating in those days. We had a fire in our room and that was it.

When we woke up on a winter's morning the ice was on the inside of the glass, not on the outside, but we didn't mind.

The house in Mingulay Street, Glasgow, that I lived in with my family

Me with my sister Carol

Me and my sister in the garden

I didn't need any toys, just a football

It was all football for me as a kid. I can't remember too many toys. All I wanted was a football.

I do remember having some Dinky toys as well, and Corgis – the cars not the dogs!

Somebody round ours had a golf club so we used to scrap about the park trying to play. A soup can in the ground was the hole for the golf.

When the Wimbledon tennis was on we would go to the public tennis courts. We hired a racquet and would try to play tennis.

It was the same when the athletics was on. We would have races round the block. We just enjoyed any sport that was flavour of the month, but I don't remember too many toys.

My first bike

I remember getting my first bike for Christmas. My dad must have saved up really hard to get me one with five-speed gears. That was us. We were up and running.

Suddenly I didn't run round the block any more, I raced around the block on my bike.

A long journey for us was probably about 10 miles on our bikes. It wasn't getting wherever we were going that was the problem – it was trying to get back!

'The ice cream man used to come on a Friday. I'd go and get an ice cream with a Cadbury's chocolate flake and watch The Third Man on the telly. Our wee treats at the end of the week were something I looked forward to'

Chocolate money

On Fridays we used to get our chocolate money – and I don't mean the stuff in gold foil. It was probably the equivalent of two-and-a-half pence.

The ice cream man used to come on a Friday. I'd go and get an ice cream with a Cadbury's chocolate flake and watch The Third Man on the telly.

I've always enjoyed chocolate and our wee treats at the end of the week were something I looked forward to.

MY BABY · SINCE I LOST MY BABY
IT'S GROWING
THE WAY YOU DO THE THINGS YOU DO

mono

IT'S THE TEMPTATIONS

Footy on the telly

Early on, we had a black and white telly. I loved Scots Sport which was the Scottish equivalent of Match of the Day. It was mostly football on that programme but very seldom did we get a live match.

I can remember Rangers playing Rapid Vienna in the European Cup in 1964. I was 13 at the time and the match was being shown on the telly.

Quite conveniently, I had the flu! My mother let me stay off school and I watched it live in the afternoon. Rangers won and funnily enough I felt better afterwards!

EUROPEAN CUP

RANGERS THROUGH

The Temptations were Tops

When I got into my teens I bought a few records.

I remember Tamla Motown records more vividly than anything else, the Four Tops, The Temptations and The Drifters, but I couldn't say I was particularly involved in music.

Football flicks 1 Going the flicks 0

A lot of kids would be into films but I didn't go to the Saturday morning cinema showings because I was always playing for the school team.

On a Saturday afternoon I would play for my amateur club so I didn't get much chance to go to the movies. Football was the priority.

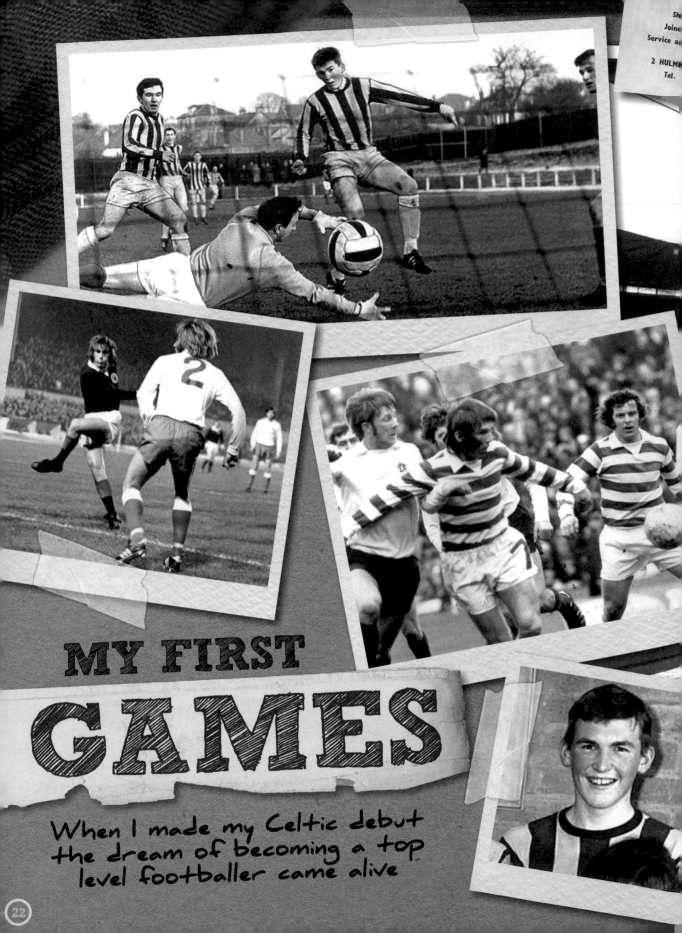

MY FIRST
GAMES

When I made my Celtic debut
the dream of becoming a top
level footballer came alive

The primary school I attended, called Miltonbank, is still there

School days

I went to a school called Miltonbank. I then managed to get a senior secondary school, High Possil Senior Secondary School.

To get to the senior side of the school must have been a mistake when they were marking my cards up! I wasn't thick at school, but I wasn't Einstein either.

My old secondary school, High Possil

J'adore fitba

My favourite subject was always Physical Education. Don't get me wrong, I enjoyed school, but it was just a way of playing competitive football for my school team.

I had a good attendance record, but I can't say I had good school reports. I remember being in secondary school and we had to get off early to train for Glasgow Schools on the other side of the city.

My school was on the north side and the training was on the south side. I used to get off a French lesson so I could get the bus and go over there in time for training.

At the end of the year, the wee French teacher said: "How many marks do you need to get past 50 in your oral?" I said five or six, and he said "I'll give you eight" so that was as well as I could do, I think.

It was football morning, noon and night, and when you got back home it was straight to the park with the kids who lived round about you.

Our school never had a football pitch. We only had a playground and had to share a pitch with one of the other schools.

When I was younger it was the same for the primary schools. We had no pitches. Then they built a new school that had one and I wanted to go there just to play on it, but I couldn't.

School goalie

Schoolboy football was always competitive, but I can't remember us organising ourselves into Celtic/ Rangers kids games. We were all mixed. It didn't affect you at that age, did it? You didn't care who anybody was. If you wanted to play football you could play, whoever you supported.

I can remember my first game for the school – they stuck me in goal. The crossbar was a long way away from me!

What was I like as a keeper? One word summed it up: Crap!

When I was at school one of the teachers, in his wisdom, also put me at centre-back as well. I was never a defender. But really, I had great encouragement from the teachers. For them to give up their time to take teams on a Saturday after working Monday to Friday takes a lot and should never be undermined or unappreciated.

In my mind, it never would be, and that goes for the guys who give up their time in the afternoons to run the amateur teams.

It's the same for the mothers who were washing the kits or darning the socks or whatever they did. It's brilliant and without that there would never be any professional football.

I'd never have made a chair-man

I left school at 15. I had a few jobs including working as a van boy, doing deliveries. I worked in a store and then got a job as a joiner, but I always wanted to be a footballer. That was my dream job.

I thought it would be best to get a trade in case I didn't make it as a footballer and that's how I ended up doing some graft as a joiner.

There was a joinery business five minutes walk from our house, so I was lucky to get a job in there. We used to work during the day and then go training at night. It did us no harm, although I wasn't very good at joinery or DIY – I had a couple of goes and wrecked a couple of chairs!

I've still got a set of tools, all wrapped up and unused. I suppose my boots were the only tools of the trade I really needed or wanted.

Turning down Bill Shankly

When I was 15, a Scottish scout came to the house and asked if I would come down to Liverpool for a few days with two or three other boys. There were trials on at night and they went well.

They asked me to come back for another fortnight so I went back down. The other lads from Glasgow were a year older than me. I asked if I could play on the same night as them. Liverpool said: "But they're a year older than you." I said: "It doesn't matter. I just want to play."

This was on the Monday, in August 1966, but they wouldn't let me, putting me down for the trial on the Tuesday with kids the same age as me instead.

Rangers were playing Celtic in the Glasgow Cup Final on the Wednesday night. I was trying to get back up the road to watch the game but I played in the trial.

Shanks and Reuben Bennett gave me a lift back to where I was staying, the YMCA on Mount Pleasant, and they said they wanted to sign me. Shanks said: "Would you be happy to come here?"

I said: "I need to go home first and see what's happening. I also need to go to West Ham as well on Saturday."

West Ham wanted to have a look at me as well, but I had really enjoyed myself at Melwood. I got on the train on the Wednesday morning and went back to Glasgow. I got to watch the match that night and Celtic won 4-0. I'd have been better staying at Anfield!

A few weeks later I went back down the road to West Ham. Ironically, they were playing Liverpool at Upton Park that day.

The players were walking out the tunnel at about quarter-to-two. The kids at West Ham used to sit behind the dugout and Shanks saw me. As I walked past him in the tunnel he shouted: "Kenny." I went bright red and just kept on walking.

So I went home knowing that West Ham wanted to sign me as well, but I was too young to be leaving Glasgow. Then Celtic came in for me and I started training there two nights a week.

It's fun to play at the YMCA...

I saw my first big football match when I was probably just four or five years of age. It was a European tie. My dad used to take me to Ibrox every week to watch Rangers. We would even go to the reserve matches as well.

I was playing for the school team and Saracen Boys Club and doing okay. A boy I knew was playing for the YMCA and he told them they should have a look at me. That's how I started to play at the next level.

They had an affiliation with Arsenal. Ian Ross, who went on to play for Liverpool, had also started at the YMCA. He went to school with my sister.

The YMCA was a really good club, so I was lucky to be asked to play for them.

I left there when I was 15 and went to play for Glasgow United and signed for Celtic when I was 16.

Future Liverpool player Ian Ross also played for the YMCA

CUMBERNAULD UNITED
Junior Football and Athletic Club

Official Opening of
Ravenswood Stadium

MONDAY 13th MAY 1968 at 7 p.m.

CUMBERNAULD UNITED

V

CELTIC

For complete coverage of all
local sport read the
CUMBERNAULD NEWS
every Thursday — 4d.

THE DAY I SIGNED FOR CELTIC

I played for a really good local team at Under 16 level. Two or three of the boys had become apprentices at Celtic so they asked if we could play them.

I scored in the game and they said they would like to sign me ahead of me possibly going to Rangers.

Jock Stein's right-hand man Sean Fallon was celebrating his wedding anniversary and he was on his way to the coast to take his wife for a treat. But he made a detour to our house and left his wife in the car while he came in for a chat.

Sean spoke to my father, who was like most dads. He'd come in from his work every night, have his tea then have a sleep on the couch or in the chair.

There were Rangers pictures on the wall at home. When Sean turned up, there was no jumping over the top of anybody to pull them down or whatever.

You always dream of playing for the team you support, but the most important thing for me was that I just wanted to be a professional footballer. Fortunately, I fulfilled my dream.

When Rangers don't take you, it's not the end of the world. It just means that when you later play against them and score, it makes it a wee bit more special.

Me, some of my Cumbernauld team-mates and club mascot Fiona Gibb

Toughening up

To toughen me up, Celtic farmed me out with about four or five other lads to a semi-professional team called Cumbernauld United.

The Scottish League at that time was full of players who were either too old to continue professional football or had been sacked from professional football because they were not good enough.

Those types of fellas often wanted to take their revenge out on somebody so when I was 16 years of age I would be getting kicked everywhere, but it was a good experience and toughened me up.

I had been sent to Cumbernauld for exactly this reason and it was a great place for me to play.

They never even had their own ground. At the end of that first season in 1968 they opened a new ground in Cumbernauld, a village which is just outside Glasgow.

It was called the Ravenswood Stadium and big Jock Stein brought Celtic along to open it. He even game me a mention in the matchday programme, saying that I was on Celtic's books.

I played for Cumbernauld and Celtic won 4-1. I think Lou Macari scored a couple, but it was a great day for the village.

On target for Cumbernauld United during my spell with the club

'I had been sent to Cumbernauld to toughen me up and it was a great place for me to play'

A Rangers fan at Celtic

A young lad by the name of Danny McGrain was at my first Celtic training session. He had been a Rangers fan as well. It didn't matter to Celtic. All they were interested in was that you could play.

Danny and I used to meet in the middle of town and get a couple of buses to training. We were always nervous in anticipation of going into training, but it was fantastic.

We trained a couple of nights a week. It was brilliant just to be part of the training. I hadn't even signed at that point.

Of course, Celtic had just won the European Cup in 1967. Just to be with the Lisbon Lions was an honour. They would ask me where I lived and pick me up in the morning and bring me into training if they could.

They would work with us. We were only 16 or 17 years of age training with these giants who had just won the European Cup. They were so humble and appreciative of what they had achieved.

They never got carried away and made us feel very welcome. I loved that about Celtic.

Danny McGrain and I were both Rangers fans who made our names at Celtic

Many years on I still look back fondly at my time at Celtic Park

Making my way, thanks to the sacrifices of others

I enjoyed a bit of success in my teens. I won a Scottish schoolboy international cap and Glasgow Schools won the Scottish Cup as well at Under 15 level. I think we were undefeated at Under 13 and Under 14 level as well.

At that stage, you don't know what is going to happen to you. You just try and enjoy it at the time.

I just prepared myself as well as I possibly could to give myself the best chance. With a wee bit of luck, you've got a chance of getting somewhere if you do that.

You are only who you are because of the people you have worked with and the people who have helped you. The first people who help you are your dad and your mum.

Without their help, guidance and sacrifices I would've found it a lot more difficult to make it as a professional footballer.

They were fantastically supportive and when I got to professional level my dad said to me: "I don't know if I will still be able to give you advice son because I am not at that level."

That's when being a professional has to kick in and it's up to you. With a little bit of luck, you can progress, but only if you give yourself the best possible chance to do so.

Shanks and big Jock

Early on during his time at Liverpool, Shanks had signed the likes of big Ronnie Yeats, Ian St John and Willie Stevenson – three Scots.

As a kid, I had seen the Saint play for Motherwell against Rangers at Ibrox. Motherwell won 5-2.

I saw Stevenson play for Rangers, but I never saw big Yeatsy play.

Ian Ross had grown up with my sister and come down to Liverpool when he was 15 or 16 so I knew he was a wee bit different and had great ability.

Shanks had this relationship with Scotland and Scottish football because a) He was Scottish, and b) Bill and his brother Bob were great friends with Jock Stein. They had a really close connection.

Shanks and Jock would meet up at big matches. They had a great affinity between them.

I think managers have the same respect between each other, but they might not have the same camaraderie.

The likes of Shankly, Stein and Matt Busby were exceptional and it goes back to their Scottish roots. A non-Scot, Don Revie, tried to jump on the back of them as well, but they were all fantastic.

Jock Stein, Billy McNeill and Bill Shankly pictured at the Celtic v Liverpool game for McNeill's testimonial in 1974

JOHN "JOCK" STEIN

5th October 1922

THE DAY I'LL NEVER FORGET

One day I will never forget was when big Jock asked me if I wanted to sign professional forms for Celtic. That's a day that means everything to me because it gave me a chance to dictate my own destiny.

From there it was up to me because I'd suddenly got the opportunity, plus all the help and support I needed, to fulfil my dreams.

'His next trial will be at the Old Bailey...'

As a teenager I was always embarrassed. If someone even said hello to me I would blush.

When I first went down to Liverpool for that first trial, we used to meet at Anfield. Everybody got changed there. We all then got on the same bus to go to the Melwood training ground.

It was brilliant. Young boys would be on the bus with the first-team players. One of them might come and stand next to you. There were no set seats. Maybe Smithy (Tommy Smith) had his own chair, but that was it. It was a great atmosphere as they made you feel comfortable.

There was always great banter on the bus. Bill Shankly would always be there. I remember a young Scottish guy came up to him in the car park and asked for a trial. Shanks explained that the trials were on that night.

The players were all winding Shanks up, saying: "He must be some player to ask you so confidently." Shanks shrugged and said: "We'll soon find out."

We came in the next day. Everyone was asking how this lad had got on. Shanks said: "The next trial he'll get will probably be at the Old Bailey."

As we got off the bus, the wee lad was there asking: "How did I do?" I can't repeat Shanks' answer. The boy must have thought he was God's gift as a footballer – it's fair to say Shankly didn't!

As a young boy, it was just great to be part of all of that. Reuben Bennett, a fellow Scot on Shankly's backroom staff, was fantastic to be around.

There was never a divide and I believe that's really important. Everything that Liverpool Football Club stands for is because of Bill Shankly.

The Quality Street Gang

Celtic had some talented young players coming through in the reserves at the time I was there.

Jock Stein had built the legendary Lisbon Lions who won the European Cup in 1967 but like Shanks at Liverpool and Bob Paisley after him, he knew the importance of building for the future. Nothing lasts forever.

That Celtic Reserve team, because of its success, was nicknamed 'The Quality Street Gang'. To be fair, that side included some of the best young players Celtic has ever produced, but we didn't get ahead of ourselves.

They included Lou Macari, Danny McGrain, David Hay, George Connelly, Paul Wilson and Vic Davidson, all very good players. We had a really good side. Other names included David Cattanach, John Gorman, Brian McLaughlin and Jimmy Quinn.

The first-team was doing well and we were successful as a reserve unit because Jock could spend a bit more time with us. A lot of people helped to improve us as individuals and team players. The staff had some really good people and we benefited from that.

Of course, Danny McGrain is still at Celtic and a few of them are still knocking about. Lou Macari came to talk to Liverpool in 1973, but ended up signing for Manchester United. There is that famous picture of Shanks coming down the stairs at Anfield with Lou ahead of him.

Shankly was fuming because the player had decided to talk to United. When my turn came in 1977, I didn't even have to think about it.

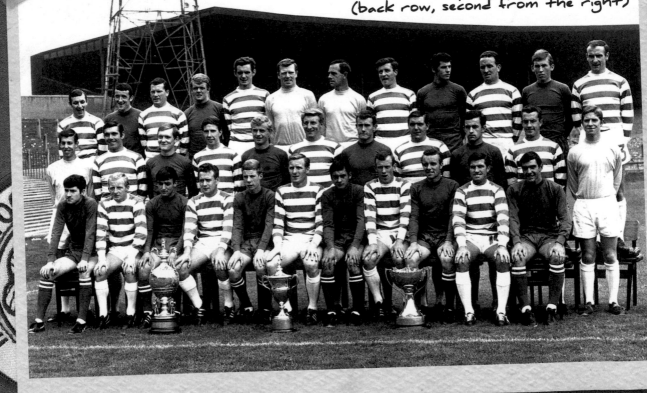

A Celtic squad photo from 1968 that includes many of the 'Quality Street Gang' and a young Kenneth Dalglish (back row, second from the right)

The Lisbon Lions –
Celtic's European Cup
winning side from 1967

David Hay

Lou Macari

George Connelly

My Celtic debut

My Celtic debut was away from home at Douglas Park in a Scottish League Cup tie, second leg, in 1968 against Hamilton Academical.

Celtic had won easily by 10 goals to nil in the first game at Celtic Park and could put a lot of youngsters in for the second leg.

We were 4-0 up at half-time and they thought they could take a chance and put me on in the second half. So I made my debut when we were 14-0 up!

My first Celtic goal in front of over 70,000 at Ibrox

In 1971 I got a regular place in the first-team at Celtic, having played three or four pre-season games and scored a few goals. The League Cup up there at that time used to be in sections.

We used to play at the start of the season in August and September – I think we played about 10 games in two months – and Celtic and Rangers were drawn in the same section.

Celtic Park was being renovated because they were putting the new stand up, so we had to play the two games on their side of town at Ibrox.

We were winning 1-0 in the first game when somebody went through and got pulled down and it was a penalty kick.

Billy McNeill said to me: "You take it." I said: "Why?" He said: "You take it. You've taken one for the reserves."

I said: "Oh, there's no difference then? Over 70,000 people and you are comparing it to reserve team football!"

It was at the Celtic end and Ibrox was as if someone had taken a knife and cut the stadium in two. One half was green and the other half was blue.

All the photographers ran behind the goal in anticipation and our fans were all cheering, although I think when they saw me stepping up they were saying 'Och no!' – or words to that effect!

It was like that moment when Alan Kennedy stepped up in the European Cup Final for Liverpool in Rome to take the final penalty and the rest of us thought 'Oh no!'

I was nervous to say the least and so knelt down to tie my laces. I finally stood and scored and that was it. I had my first Celtic goal.

Old Firm or not - you always need passion

We played Rangers three times in six weeks at Ibrox in 1971 and we beat them every time.

People talk about the passion of the Old Firm at Celtic Park and Ibrox but I don't think it matters where the venue is you're playing at. You should always have passion.

You might not be good enough, but that doesn't mean you cannot apply yourself properly and see where that takes you. Your level of ability doesn't matter. It's your application that counts first.

I was lucky. Celtic under big Jock was fantastic for me. Then coming to Liverpool with old Bob, you couldn't get any better, could you?

Celtic FC total games and goals

ERA	GAMES	GOALS
1968-69	1	0
1969-70	4	0
1970-71	6	0
1971-72	53	29
1972-73	56	39
1973-74	59	25
1974-75	51	21
1975-76	53	32
1976-77	54	27
TOTAL	337	173

Scoring for the Tartan Army

I made my senior international debut for Scotland in a 1-0 win against Belgium in 1971 when I came on as sub in a Euro '72 qualifier. It was great for me. I had played in the Under 23 team, but this was my first senior cap.

Tommy Docherty was the Scottish manager and he was a really good character but he left the job to go to Man United in 1972. He couldn't have been too happy with the way I was playing then because he never asked me to go to Old Trafford!

My first goal for Scotland was in 1972 against Denmark at Hampden Park where they used to have Celtic and Rangers ends for Scotland games. I scored at the Celtic end.

George Graham squared it across to me and I just swung my left leg at it and it ended up in the net. I was happy for myself, but I also remembered the sacrifices my parents had made for me.

My dad went everywhere watching me playing. My mother never came. She wasn't allowed, probably due to superstition or whatever.

As a young boy growing up, everyone dreams about scoring for their country. When you actually do it, it's a fantastic feeling.

My first Scotland goal came in this match against Denmark in 1972

LIVERPOOL FOOTBALL CLUB

LIVERPOOL FOOTBALL CLUB

THE KOP
ARE TOP

Liverpool

LIVERPOOL

40

A drive to Anfield and the drive to win

I will never forget my Celtic career and what they did for me. In my time there we won four Scottish titles, four Scottish Cups and one Scottish League Cup.

In 1977, when I was 26, it was time to think about the next phase in my career. The place I had always wanted to go to was Liverpool because I'd been down there at 15 and saw exactly what it was like.

I watched a documentary after they got beaten by Manchester United in the 1977 FA Cup Final. Liverpool had won the league and they put that Wembley defeat behind them to go on and win the European Cup in Rome, beating Borussia Moenchengladbach.

Kevin Keegan was leaving and I hoped that they would come in for me after that. As soon as they did, I was delighted.

There was no tapping anybody up. We had been playing in a friendly at Dunfermline on the Tuesday night. I got a phone call after the game. I was at my father-in-law's pub. It was big Jock. He said: "I'm at the ground. Do you still want to go?" I said: "Yes."

He said: "Liverpool and Bob Paisley are here if you want to talk to them."

I drove up and spoke to Bob and John Smith. They had been at the game at Dunfermline and had come back to Celtic Park. The conversation lasted about five minutes and then I arranged to meet them in the morning so they could drive us back to Liverpool.

Jock took me down to Moffat in southern Scotland and dropped us off at the hotel. Bob and John Smith took me back for the medical and I signed on the Wednesday.

I was the luckiest man in the world to be in a position to be able to go where I wanted to go with the team I now wanted to play for.

Old Bob was brilliant. I came into Anfield and it was similar to what had happened when I was 16 years of age going to Celtic when they had just won the European Cup.

The players were hungry to win another one. The main reason I joined Liverpool was to win things, something they'd been used to.

The great thing was, no matter how many things they had won, it never made them any less hungry to drive on and win something else.

Secret of Liverpool's success

In the 1970s Liverpool was the best run football club in England. There was no-one who was any better than club secretary Peter Robinson.

Chairman John Smith obviously benefited from Peter's knowledge and Liverpool Football Club had the best manager in old Bob.

The fans had always been there and you should never take for granted what that means to a club. We knew that as long as you were out there on the pitch giving it everything, then those fans would support you. All you had to do was play.

Everything else was in order. They used to talk about the secret of Liverpool's success. It's not a secret. You just get the best people you possibly can, play them in their best positions and take it from there. If you do that, you've got a chance. That's what they did.

It all sounds so simple. The club was superbly run. Everybody loved playing for Liverpool and the way they treated their players was unbelievable.

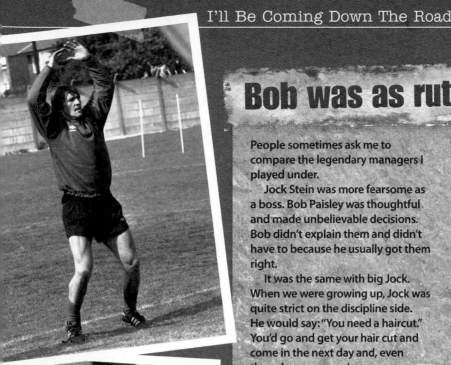

Bob was as ruthless as Jock

People sometimes ask me to compare the legendary managers I played under.

Jock Stein was more fearsome as a boss. Bob Paisley was thoughtful and made unbelievable decisions. Bob didn't explain them and didn't have to because he usually got them right.

It was the same with big Jock. When we were growing up, Jock was quite strict on the discipline side. He would say: "You need a haircut." You'd go and get your hair cut and come in the next day and, even though we were only on young boys' wages, he'd say "you did not get enough off. Go back again."

I suppose it was measured, but also, when you saw him away from the football, he was a caring man as well. He cared for you, he respected you, he was grateful for what you did, but he never let his guard down when he was working.

Old Bob was friendly and great with everybody, but was never afraid to make a ruthless decision.

I remember when he left out Terry Mac saying 'he's injured'. Terry had a sore thumb.

Bob was fantastic. I don't know how he made some of those decisions. It might have been instinct or intuition, but whatever it was he made so many correct calls.

That's why Liverpool had their most successful time under him.

MY FIRST MELWOOD TRAINING SESSION

Replacing Kevin Keegan

Kevin Keegan was a fantastic player for Liverpool and won the game's biggest honours. Then he left for Hamburg where he won the German title and the European Footballer of the Year. That tells you something about Kevin as a player.

But it wasn't my problem that Kevin wanted to leave. It was to my benefit. If you are going to come in and play, be yourself. I didn't want to try and be Kevin Keegan.

I was always taught: 'Just be yourself and if you are good enough, everybody will be happy. If you are not, well, okay, you have tried your best and it has just not worked out.'

Kevin Keegan shows off the Football Writers' Footballer of the Year trophy in 1976

Head to head with Keegan as Scotland played England at Wembley in 1979

Liverpool's number seven shirt

I was handed Kevin's famous number 7 shirt when I joined Liverpool.

Yes, it's a special number at Anfield because the likes of Ian Callaghan also wore it, but any shirt should not be a noose around the neck of the person wearing it because of the greats who went before. It should be an honour to wear it.

The Liverpool number 7 shirt is not heavier than any of the others. That's your number, do your best, be yourself.

It will live on forever.

It was an honour to wear the number 7 shirt I inherited from Kevin Keegan

It didn't take long for me to be accepted in the number seven shirt

My first

YOU'LL NEVER WALK ALONE

LIVERPOOL

games

A Wembley debut

After signing for Liverpool I trained on the Thursday morning with the players. It turned out my debut was at Wembley in the Charity Shield which is the reward you get for the work you have done the previous season. I had not contributed to that because I had not been there.

They had won the European Cup and the League Championship in 1977 so we were going to London to play against Manchester United.

Wembley is a fabulous arena to go and play in. The Charity Shield was a reflection of what you had achieved the year before. Let's just say I was basking in reflected glory. It was a nice place to go and bask.

It was a fantastic curtain raiser. I don't remember too much about the game, apart from getting cramp! It was nice for me to get in and play the first game for my new club at Wembley.

We drew 0-0 with United. It's not trying to undermine Wembley, but the first big game for me was going to be at Anfield.

I was closely marked during my first game for Liverpool against old rivals Manchester United

A tight game at Wembley finished 0-0 so I didn't manage to mark my debut with a goal

1977

48

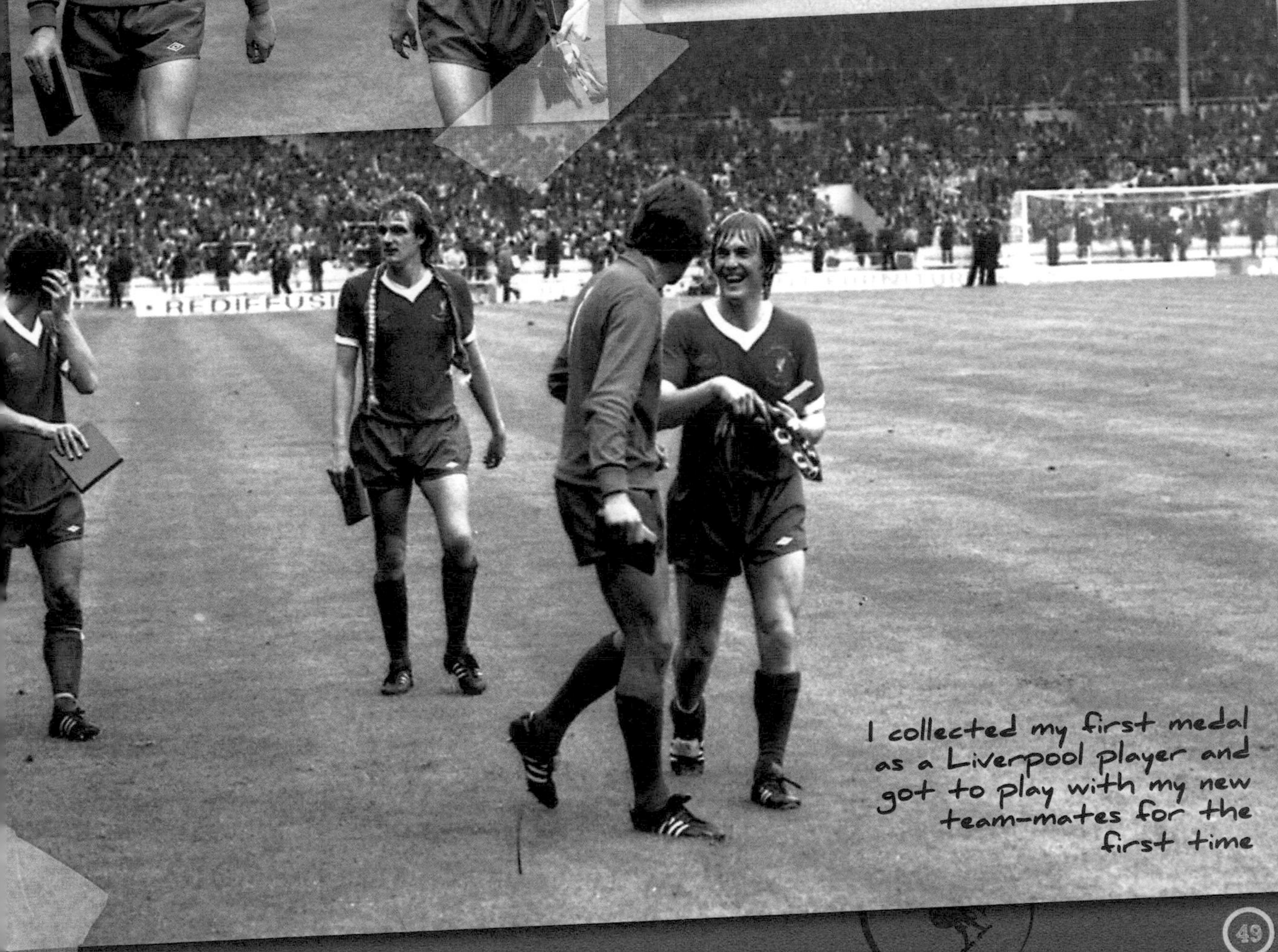

I collected my first medal as a Liverpool player and got to play with my new team-mates for the first time

First goal for Liverpool

I scored on my league debut at Middlesbrough with compliments to Terry McDermott. Graeme Souness was playing against us. He tried to leave his mark on me, of course, but let's just say he caught my elbow!

My Anfield debut was against Newcastle. There was a boy playing for them called Tommy Craig.

We had grown up together at schoolboy level, Under 13, 14 and 15 Glasgow Schools and Scottish Schoolboys. We were coming out on the pitch at Anfield about five minutes before the game.

I said to wee Tommy: "That sign up there is supposed to make you nervous." He said: "If it's making you nervous, you should see what it's doing to me." It was the first time I had ever touched the This is Anfield sign.

In the second half, Ray Kennedy played a ball through to me and I ran on towards the Kop and put it in the back of the net. I was up and running and what a fantastic feeling that was.

A league debut at Ayresome Park in Middlesbrough also saw my first Liverpool goal in a 1-1 draw

Learning the Liverpool Way right from the start

I sensed Liverpool were good winners as soon as I arrived at Anfield. Winning never affected their hunger for future success.

If you come to a football club you want to be successful and coming to Liverpool was giving me a really good chance. The attitude of the players was a huge contribution towards that.

We went on to win a few league titles and each and every one of them was equally enjoyable. The best one was probably the last one because it was the most recent. There are a lot of medals there. A lot of success and a lot of memories.

Ronnie Moran used to come with the medals in a shoe box. He would say: "There you are. The League Championship medals are there. If you think you deserve it, take one."

Whether you deserved it or not, you took one. I certainly took one. That was their way of saying 'you got your reward for last year, now let's start again'.

There was no fanfare for the celebrations, but I tell you, we knew how to celebrate. We knew how to enjoy it, but it never took away any of the hunger for the following season.

When we started off they used to say: 'As long as we're in the Charity Shield next year'. That would mean we had enjoyed a good season and won the league or the cup, or both, or just been pipped for both and got in because someone else had won the double.

Fortunately for us it was usually because we had done well.

I'd love to watch a game from **THE KOP.**

I'm hoping to sneak on there, anonymously!

The thing about the Kop is that you wanted to be in there, but you couldn't because you were playing. I wanted to get in there and experience it.

I have a real understanding of what it must have meant to the likes of Phil Thompson and Tommy Smith who had stood on the Kop as kids and then been able to come out and play in front of them. It must have been unbelievable for people like that.

The closest I ever got was my son Paul being in there. A guy used to keep him his speck and he used to stand on the Kop and watch the games. I would have loved to have done that.

I nearly fell in there a couple of times. I remember scoring against Tottenham and Ray Clemence in 1982 when we won the

Championship. We won 3-1 that day, Ronnie Whelan got the last goal.

I was nearly over the Kop barrier in that match so I have been close to it a couple of times. It's just something that I would have loved to have done.

The only time I was on the Kop properly was after Hillsborough. I walked through with the kids. Since then I've sat in The Kop for a number of Hillsborough anniversary services, but never for a game.

I know Bill Shankly once stood on the Kop when he retired. Who knows? Maybe one day I'll get there for a big game...but there might not be any tickets!

I'd like to do it anonymously. I wouldn't want to do it with a fanfare or for any PR or publicity.

I would just love to be in there with the fans who have always chanted my name.

Don't forget, the Kop have never lost a game. We've lost a few on the pitch, but they have never lost a single match.

‘We won 3-1 against Spurs in 1982. I was nearly over the Kop barrier in that match’

The KING'S HONOURS

From playing my first games
with Celtic and Scotland to making
my name throughout Europe with my
Liverpool team-mates, we're all in the
game for one reason — to win medals.
Let me take you through my
personal collection...

The most famous dink ever...on the biggest stage

My goal against Bruges at Wembley in the 1978 European Cup final wasn't that difficult really.

As soon as I went through and was one on one with the goalie I knew what I was going to do.

Before that goal, when Terry Mac went through, the keeper went down early so I knew he was going to go to ground. It was up to me then.

I knew what he was going to do and it was just as well I knew what I was going to do because we only won 1-0!

European Cup Final –
Liverpool v AS Roma
30th May, 1984

European Cup Final –
Liverpool v Real Madrid.
27th May, 1981

DECEMBER 13th, 1981
1 9 8 1
NATIONAL STADIUM
TOKYO JAPAN
PRESENTED
By
TOYOTA

The Toyota World Club Championship medal from 1981

COUPE DES CLUBS CHAMPIONS EUROPEENS

1985

European Cup Final – Liverpool v Juventus 29th May, 1985

European glory

There were two things that made it very attractive to come to Liverpool. One was to win domestic trophies, but the big prize was to have a chance to collect European trophies.

We got to the semi-final of the European Cup a couple of times when I was with Celtic, but to come down to Liverpool in my first season and walk away with the European Cup was unbelievable.

I could not have picked a better club with a better pedigree to come and try to achieve that aim of winning European trophies.

To win the European Cup in my first year was something I was very fortunate to have achieved. I don't think the game itself would have been classed as one of the best European Cup finals by the neutrals, but it was for us.

We were playing Bruges and they had a few suspensions so their team was weakened. But it doesn't matter who you are playing. There are still eleven in front of you. You've got to beat them and we did 1-0. That was good enough and it was unbelievable.

I must have been excited because after I scored, I jumped the advertising boards. I thought of the 1974 Commonwealth Games after scoring when Alan Pascoe won the 400 metres hurdles.

On his lap of honour he tried to jump a hurdle and fell. I jumped it going one way, so I wasn't going to jump it coming back, so I stepped over. But to score was a dream come true.

For me it didn't matter who scored. If David Fairclough had tapped it into the net, that would have been no problem for me. We just wanted that trophy and having tasted it once, you wanted it again.

That is a great reflection of the players at Liverpool Football Club. When they won a European Cup the year before, it only whetted their appetite to go out and win it more often.

All we did was apply the same mentality of the players that were here the year before and looked forward to doing it again.

Nobody ever got carried away with the success they achieved at Anfield or Celtic Park. I was lucky that in both of my first seasons, with Celtic and Liverpool – I picked up a couple of medals for both clubs.

Enjoying an open top bus ride

It's a great honour to captain any football club, but certainly to lead one as prestigious as Celtic had been very special. I did it for two or three years. In my last year, we won the double.

The only thing about winning trophies in Glasgow is that you can't do a tour of the city because of the atmosphere between the Celtic and Rangers fans.

When I came to Liverpool I was able to experience all the fans lining the streets – it was a remarkable thing. The welcome we got in 1978 after beating Bruges at Wembley to win the European Cup typified it.

It was slightly different in 1986 when we did the double at Liverpool. We never actually got to celebrate on the coach journey home from Chelsea after winning the league at Stamford Bridge because Alan Hansen, Steve Nicol and myself were going to Glasgow, but we had an opportunity the following week when we were back at Wembley to play Everton in the first all-Merseyside FA Cup final.

After pipping Everton for the league, they were up for it, so we had to match their effort and commitment in the first half when we were 1-0 down.

In the second half we played more like we had played for the latter part of the season and ended up winning 3-1 so the celebrations we missed out on the week before were made up for on the Saturday night.

'In 1986 we never actually got to celebrate on the coach journey home from Chelsea after winning the league because a few of us had to head to Glasgow, but we had an opportunity the following week. We were at Wembley to play Everton in the FA Cup final and ended up winning 3-1. The celebrations we missed out on the week before were made up for on the Saturday night'

The two medals I got in a week in May 1986

Individual honours but part of a team

I was named as PFA Player of the Year in 1983 and Football Writers' Footballer of the Year in 1979 and 1983.

Obviously, the PFA awards are voted for by your fellow professionals and it's always nice to get recognition from the players you compete against for the game's big honours.

The country's elite football writers name the annual Footballer of the Year. This was first won by the legendary Stanley Matthews in 1948. Amazingly, he won it again 15 years later. It has all the game's greatest names on the trophy and so it is a real honour if you win it.

But let's be clear. It recognises what your team has achieved rather than what you have achieved as an individual.

You can never win anything without the rest of your team. It's nice to have the award and the accolade, but it's never an individual thing. Three winners medals is always more important at the end of the season than one individual award.

Getting something like the Footballer of the Year award from the game's top football writers is interesting because during the season they can be criticising you and praising you at the same time.

Again, the award makes you feel very humble, but it's only an indication of how successful your team has been. You are only part of that team.

A Football Writers' Association award recognising all of Liverpool's players in 1989

Football Writers' Association F.O.T.Y. award winners

1947–48	Stanley Matthews	Blackpool
1948–49	Johnny Carey	Manchester United
1949–50	Joe Mercer	Arsenal
1950–51	Harry Johnston	Blackpool
1951–52	Billy Wright	Wolves
1952–53	Nat Lofthouse	Bolton Wanderers
1953–54	Tom Finney	Preston North End
1954–55	Don Revie	Manchester City
1955–56	Bert Trautmann	Manchester City
1956–57	Tom Finney	Preston North End
1957–58	Danny Blanchflower	Tottenham Hotspur
1958–59	Syd Owen	Luton Town
1959–60	Bill Slater	Wolves
1960–61	Danny Blanchflower	Tottenham Hotspur
1961–62	Jimmy Adamson	Burnley
1962–63	Stanley Matthews	Stoke City
1963–64	Bobby Moore	West Ham United
1964–65	Bobby Collins	Leeds United
1965–66	Bobby Charlton	Manchester United
1966–67	Jack Charlton	Leeds United
1967–68	George Best	Manchester United
1968–69	Tony Book (joint winner)	Manchester City
1968–69	Dave Mackay (joint winner)	Derby County
1969–70	Billy Bremner	Leeds United
1970–71	Frank McLintock	Arsenal
1971–72	Gordon Banks	Stoke City
1972–73	Pat Jennings	Tottenham Hotspur
1973–74	Ian Callaghan	Liverpool
1974–75	Alan Mullery	Fulham
1975–76	Kevin Keegan	Liverpool
1976–77	Emlyn Hughes	Liverpool
1977–78	Kenny Burns	Nottingham Forest
1978–79	**Kenny Dalglish**	**Liverpool**
1979–80	Terry McDermott	Liverpool
1980–81	Frans Thijssen	Ipswich Town
1981–82	Steve Perryman	Tottenham Hotspur
1982–83	**Kenny Dalglish**	**Liverpool**
1983–84	Ian Rush	Liverpool
1984–85	Neville Southall	Everton
1985–86	Gary Lineker	Everton
1986–87	Clive Allen	Tottenham Hotspur
1987–88	John Barnes	Liverpool
1988–89	Steve Nicol	Liverpool
1989–90	John Barnes	Liverpool
1990–91	Gordon Strachan	Leeds United
1991–92	Gary Lineker	Tottenham Hotspur
1992–93	Chris Waddle	Sheffield Wed
1993–94	Alan Shearer	Blackburn Rovers
1994–95	Jurgen Klinsmann	Tottenham Hotspur
1995–96	Eric Cantona	Manchester United
1996–97	Gianfranco Zola	Chelsea
1997–98	Dennis Bergkamp	Arsenal
1998–99	David Ginola	Tottenham Hotspur
1999–00	Roy Keane	Manchester United
2000–01	Teddy Sheringham	Manchester United
2001–02	Robert Pires	Arsenal
2002–03	Thierry Henry	Arsenal
2003–04	Thierry Henry	Arsenal
2004–05	Frank Lampard	Chelsea
2005–06	Thierry Henry	Arsenal
2006–07	Cristiano Ronaldo	Manchester United
2007–08	Cristiano Ronaldo	Manchester United
2008–09	Steven Gerrard	Liverpool
2009–10	Wayne Rooney	Manchester United
2010–11	Scott Parker	West Ham United
2011–12	Robin van Persie	Arsenal
2012–13	Gareth Bale	Tottenham Hotspur

Liverpool players have won the Footballer of the Year award 11 times – more than any other club

1986

Managers are not one-man bands

For me, winning the Manager of the Year award three times at Liverpool was always a reflection of the work done by people like Ronnie Moran and Roy Evans.

They were totally supportive, and then there was Peter Robinson upstairs, the board, the players and the fans.

Everybody should share in any success because everybody has made a contribution. I was just the person who had to stand there and accept the award.

I'm very fortunate, but I've never been a one-man band. You will never get any success if you think you are more important than anybody else.

You only get a Manager of the Year award if your team is successful. And there is more than one person in a team.

Being a manager is hugely different to being a player. As a player your preparation is all about

1988

1990

yourself. You do a little bit of homework on the opposition, or at least I did as a player.

As a manager you have to do your homework on the opposition. You have to do the homework on your own players. You have to make sure everything is right during the week.

You are not just worrying about yourself, so the success as a team is hugely rewarding and satisfying.

To win awards as a manager doesn't feel any different to winning them as a player. I still felt I was part of them and I think that is the way it should be. There should be the same feeling of privilege and pride to win any award. You won't win if you are carrying passengers in any way, shape or form.

As a manager, you have decisions to make that are sometimes not very pleasant. But then it's not pleasant when you come away on a Saturday and you have lost a game.

The most important thing for me when it came to making decisions was simple. Do you want to be a winner on the day, or do you want to shirk a decision that might cost you?

Everyone wants to play. A manager has to make a harsh decision about who is going to play and who isn't. As long as a manager has his reasons, people might be unhappy, but on reflection they might understand it.

It's amazing when that happens as a player. Your thoughts about a manager might have some foundation or they might not. But usually, when you look into the mirror and if you are honest enough, you might understand why the manager made those decisions on the day. The most important thing is the team, more important than any individual.

That's the way I was brought up at Liverpool. There was no player who was any bigger there or appreciated more than any other. The manager was always totally respected and respectful of the players until you did something wrong.

That is your own fault. Everyone was seen as an equal. Everyone was treated as an equal. This contributed to the success we had.

I don't know if, as a manager, you find things out about yourself that you never thought you had, but you just adjust to things and move on through the various guises, always aware that the best job you could ever have was as a player.

There is no such person as Peter Pan. You have to finish some time.

Clutching the Daily Mirror Man of the Decade award for the 1980s

We had a high level of interest in collecting Barclays awards too!

65

My first trophies

I was lucky enough to come in and be a part of Celtic's double-winning team in 1971/72, my first senior medals. It's always important to win trophies.

Celtic Football Club has always been expected to win trophies, but then so have Rangers. There has always been this huge rivalry and intense pressure for those teams to deliver.

There might only be two or three teams up there capable of winning the title, but it's still a hell of an achievement.

You can't be too disappointed when you come into the team and walk away with two trophies in your first season and I certainly wasn't.

Scottish Football Association

Winners
Scottish Cup
1971-72

FIRST DIVISION
Season
1971-72
To Dad from Ken

Nutmegging Clem!

My favourite memory of playing for Scotland is maybe scoring against England at Hampden – only because it went through Clem's legs!

Another big one would have to be when I scored the goal to equal Denis' record against Spain in a World Cup qualifier in November 1984. It went into the top corner and we beat them 3-1.

I turned after scoring and ran towards the crowd. My old man was on the front row and I saw him. He was up out of his seat, cheering. It doesn't get much better than that.

A special cap from Franz Beckenbauer

My hero Denis Law

Proud to share a goals record with Denis Law

I share the Scotland international goals record with Denis Law.

We both got 30 goals although the Scottish FA chopped off one I scored against Wales, declaring it was an own goal.

It was going in anyway, but I would share anything with Denis who was one of my heroes when I was growing up. He's a fantastic fella and so to share the Scottish international goals record with him is very humbling and special.

To get 102 Scotland caps is a bit of a reflection of Scottish football at that time and the relative success we had in qualifying for three World Cups in a row which, for us, was really successful.

When we got there we never did much, but reaching the finals was a real achievement for a small country.

I'm very proud of my 102 caps and the fact that it is still a record.

As long as it says 'winners' on it, that's all that matters

I don't know why they changed the style from plaques to gold medals for winning the league.

This one was for the first league championship I won with Liverpool in 1978/79. The first year I was at Liverpool we won the European Cup, the second year we came away with the league championship.

It's amazing when you look at the differences. By 1981/82 the plaques had gone and we were receiving medals. I don't know whether it was down to cut-backs or modern technology!

In their own way they are both a fantastic recognition of what we achieved at Liverpool Football Club.

As an individual, it doesn't matter to me whether they look like this early one or the later one. The most important thing is that it's engraved 'Winners'.

That is what we went out to do and what we were fortunate enough to have done a few times.

Both medals are very pleasant on the eye, especially when you have helped to win them.

Receiving the MBE

In 1984 I was awarded an MBE. I was a footballer who was living the dream of a wee boy, having been able to play for two fantastic football clubs. I was playing for Scotland at the time and they were a great team as well. You just did what you did and didn't look for recognition.

To get an award like that from the Queen is great for your family. It was tremendous to take the two kids down to Buckingham Palace in early 1985 to collect it, although I don't think Kelly and Paul would be too happy looking at the pictures of them down there!

We came back and the next night Liverpool beat York City 7-0 in the FA Cup, so that made it even better.

'To get an award like that from the Queen is great for your family. It was tremendous to take the two kids down to Buckingham Palace in early 1985 to collect it'

1. UEFA Super Cup winners medal (1977 v Hamburg). 2. UEFA Super Cup runners-up medal (1984 v Juventus). 3. League Cup winners medals from 1981-84. 4. FA Cup winners medal (1986 v Everton). 5. 1989 FA Cup semi-final medal (v Nottingham Forest). 6. Dubai Super Cup winners medal (1986 v Celtic). 7. 1974 Day of German Unity medal collected while playing for Scotland. 8. Drybrough Cup runners-up medal (1971 v Aberdeen). 9. A special Kenny Dalglish garden gnome. 10. League championship trophy. 11. With the Liverpool ECHO Sports Personality of the Year award won in 1979 and 1980.

LIVERPOOL
KENNY DALGLISH

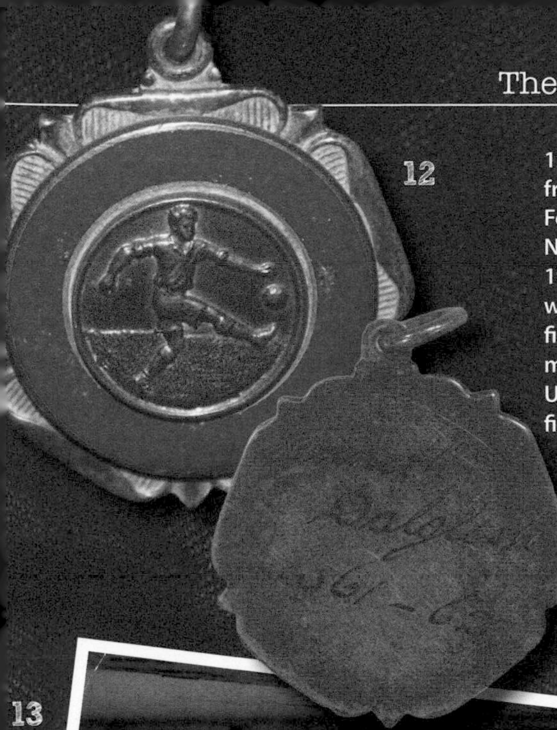

12

13

12. Schoolboy football medal from 1961-62. 13. With the Football Writers' Association North Managers Award from 1986. 14. Eight Charity Shield winners medals – including his first LFC medal from the 1977 match against Manchester United. 15. Littlewoods Cup finalist trophy (1987 v Arsenal). 16. A cap from the British Home Championships in May 1974. 17. The medals I won during my time at Celtic. 18. The Queen's Silver Jubilee Cup that was contested for by a Glasgow XI and a Football League XI

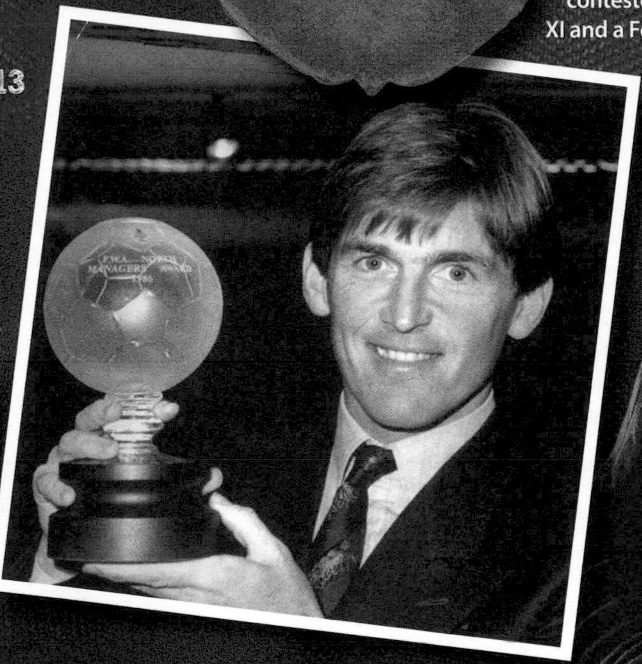

14

PHOTO ALBUM

I've shown you my medals and now I've got some photos for you to see.
You've probably seen a lot of shots of me before but this unique collection includes a few from my family album and lots that make me smile

Eric Morecambe keeps me laughing as he hands over an award in May 1983

The feeling of winning my first league title as player-manager is etched all over my face on May 3, 1986

With Alex Ferguson in December 1986 conducting a radio phone-in about our respective clubs

Suited up with my ex-Scotland boss Tommy Docherty and Anfield legend Bob Paisley

Opening a tea bar at Liverpool Maternity Hospital in 1985 with Marina

A picture from my league debut for Liverpool at Middlesbrough. The game got off to the best possible start for me as I scored after just seven minutes, but the game finished 1-1

With Marina, Kelly and Paul around the time of my transfer to Liverpool

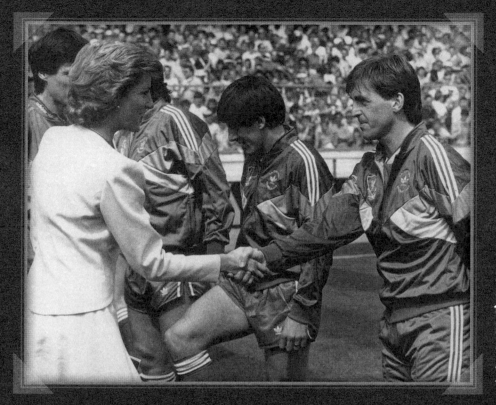

Shaking hands with Princess Diana before the 1988 FA Cup final. It was all downhill after that

Pushing over a pile of pennies (I was told to!) in the Albany pub in Liverpool in 1980 that were collected for the Royal National Institute for the Blind

I got the chance to introduce Queen Elizabeth II to members of a Glasgow Select XI before a match against a Football League XI at Hampden Park. The match was in aid of the Silver Jubilee Appeal in 1977

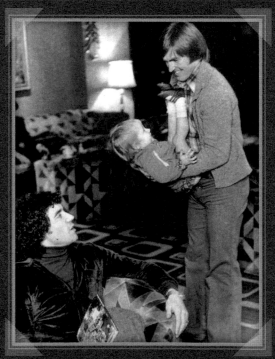

I bumped into Kevin Keegan in a Liverpool hotel shortly after I replaced him in the Reds' number seven shirt. My daughter Kelly was only interested in playing with Daddy

Not only did I take part in the record, but I had to sell it as well! It was for a good cause though as 'He Ain't Heavy, He's My Brother' in aid of the Hillsborough charities became the Christmas number one in 2012

I get a hug for my troubles from one excited fan in an Eighties-style jumper as we beat Spurs 3-1 in May 1982 to secure the championship

As you may know, I'm partial to a round of golf. Here I am carrying my clubs at Childwall Golf Club during the Hillsborough Memorial event in 2004

I may look like I'm preparing for a career as a butcher but I'm actually at the Barr Company soft drinks factory in Atherton, Lancashire. They make the famous "Irn Bru" drink

I was under close scrutiny as I made my Liverpool debut against Manchester United at Wembley in August 1977

Here's the whole clan pictured shortly after Lauren's birth in 1988

84

I swapped shirts after a friendly with Argentina
in Buenos Aires in 1977 which ended 1-1

Me, Marina and Koppy the Superlambanana at St George's Hall in 2008

Who says men can't show emotion? I'm every bit as proud of Marina as she is of me

Rafa Benitez hands me the Bill Shankly Memorial Award at the ECHO Sports Personality of the Year event in 2007

The joy of scoring a goal is obvious after I netted against Sunderland in the FA Cup fourth round in 1982. I got two in a 3-0 win

It's Liverpool against Everton again...this time in aid of Marina's charity in 2006

Don't be fooled. It's not Father Christmas. It's me...raising money for charity during a Santa Dash

SHIRTS, BOOTS & BALLS

Shirt designs don't matter – at least if you've got one you know you are in the team!

When I was at Celtic we didn't have numbers on our shirts, only on the shorts, and the simpler you keep it the better for me.

There were not particularly any really horrendous kits that I played in during my career.

Maybe there was a yellow one with red squiggles through it at Liverpool that could've been better, but in those days as long as you were wearing a Liverpool shirt with a number that was below 12 you were happy because you knew you were playing.

Idolising Denis Law

When I was growing up, most of the kids would idolise Denis Law. Then there was the great Rangers player Jim Baxter and Celtic's Jimmy Johnstone.

Depending on who you supported, you had your own Celtic and Rangers heroes, but Denis was right up there for me.

Denis Law's shirt

I played in a testimonial game for Bobby Charlton, Manchester United v Celtic. Denis Law played for Man U.

The only thing is he was wearing a number eight shirt when his famous number was 10, but I ran up the tunnel after him anyway and he gave me his shirt.

Big Jock Stein said to me afterwards: "We're giving our set of shirts to charity." I said to Jock: "How much do you want because you're not getting that one."

Footballers swap many shirts these days, but Denis Law's shirt was good enough for me.

Me, Denis Law and the Scotland World Cup squad in 1974 recording a song for the West Germany World Cup

The yellow jersey

I don't really remember my first school jersey. It might have been yellow because I was in goal! I was never a goalkeeper, though. I knew that.

I eventually got to play in the same Scotland team as Denis Law — and even recorded a World Cup song with him and the rest of the lads!

It's all in the stripes — but do those expensive boots really make you play better?

As a kid, the first boots I remember getting were probably the big brown leather ones with no markings on them. I think they were called Hotspurs.

They had studs with nails in them and you had to hammer them in. I used to wear them in the street.

The nails would come up through the sole. You would take your sock off and there would be a hole in it. They were the boots with the big solid toecaps.

Then I would go for a boot that was a copy of a famous make. The more expensive adidas boots had three stripes but we would have to go to Timpson's.

Their boots had four stripes, but they were half the price. Or I would get Puma with the slash that went one way.

If you went to the Co-operative store you could get St Crispin Wings boots with the stripe going the other way. We thought they were Pumas.

The first branded boots I had was a pair of Pumas, given to me as a kid when I went on trial to West Ham.

Head cases

I hear lots of criticism these days about modern balls.

All the critics need to do is get hold of one of those old leather balls with the lace on it, soak it in the bath, throw it in the air then challenge any modern player to jump up and head it.

My advice would be just try and avoid the lace. They were very heavy and if you caught the lace it could open up a cut on your forehead.

The balls and the technology around them moves on. They keep trying to change things and it makes it hard for the goalkeepers because they do move a lot more in the air these days.

People want to see more goals, but they have to be a little bit fairer on the goalkeepers – a view that might have been very different when I was playing!

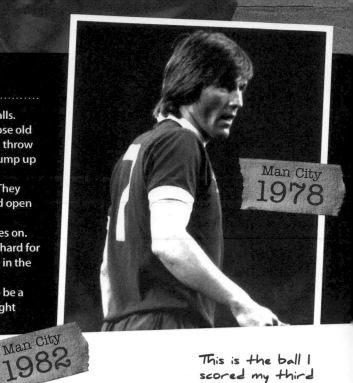

Man City
1978

Man City
1982

Man City
1978

Wrexham
1978

This is the ball I scored my third LFC hat-trick with

Official
World Cup Ball
1982

adidas
Made

Hand Sewn

Hat-trick ball

I didn't score too many hat-tricks. I got
three for Liverpool and two were against
Manchester City. The other was against
Wrexham. I used to stop at two goals!

It's interesting when you look back at the
way the balls changed. This Tango ball, the
one I scored my second hat-trick against City
with, started to be used around 1982, but it is
still very different from the old laced brown
leather balls we would use.

In the old League Cup finals, they used
to have a Mitre ball with red lines running
through it. You couldn't see it – it was almost
hypnotising you!

Then we moved on again with different
footballs for different competitions and
different manufacturers sponsoring big
competitions. Most of the teams now train
with the ball that they are going to be playing
with in the next game.

We have seen the evolution of the modern ball. It's great for the players when they take free-kicks, as long as it's for you and not against you.

They have really got into it technically and I don't know if it's for the better or not. I think if you want to bend a football, bend it using your ability, not because the manufacturers have made it easier to bend it. But I suppose it all adds to the excitement.

The best of it is that most of us wanted to make it difficult for the goalkeepers, although if I had hit the target a bit more often I might have scored a few more hat-tricks and collected more balls like that adidas Tango one!

Man City
1982

Man City
1982

Man City
1982

Man City
1982

Man City
1982

Man City
1982

AWAY DAYS

In many ways Anfield became the focus of my life, but I've enjoyed other places too with legends like Souey...

MY FAVOURITE OTHER GROUNDS

My favourite ground would have to be **Wembley** because it was normally a final when we played there and that meant we had enjoyed a good season.

There is no particular club ground that stands out. I was just happy to go and play anywhere. You were just lucky to be playing football on a Saturday.

Everywhere we went there was always a decent atmosphere. **Goodison Park** was always a fantastic place for the derbies, but then everybody has their own derbies.

The great thing about Liverpool is that when the two big clubs play each other, fans can go to the game together.

It's not as good as it used to be. There is a bit more venom these days, but the vast majority of fans should still be applauded for the way they conduct themselves before, during and after the matches.

The city of Liverpool should be really proud of these traditions.

A Wembley win in the League Cup against Manchester United in 1983

Liverpool and Everton fans stand together at Wembley in 1986

KENNY'S GOT DOUBLE VISION

Wembley League Cup finals in 1984 (left) and 1983 (right)

LIVERPOOL FC

LIVERPOOL PRIDE OF MERSEYSIDE

EVERTON 0   LIVERPOOL 2

I always enjoyed the atmosphere at Goodison derbies — especially when I scored like in this 3-2 win from 1985

My favourite European trips: Paris and Rome

You wouldn't be surprised if I said Paris '81 and Rome '84 were my favourite away European trips with Liverpool, but we were not there to enjoy the scenery.

We were there to win the games. We did that in both Paris and Rome and really enjoyed it. You can't beat getting a winners' medal at the end of a game, especially if it's a European Cup winners' medal.

I don't remember much about the parties afterwards, unlike Bob Paisley at Rome in '77. I should've done what he did, which was to ensure he soaked it all up. He never took a drink, old Bob, saying that he just wanted to get drunk on the atmosphere.

I never listened to his advice on that!

Paris '81 saw my first European Cup win on foreign soil

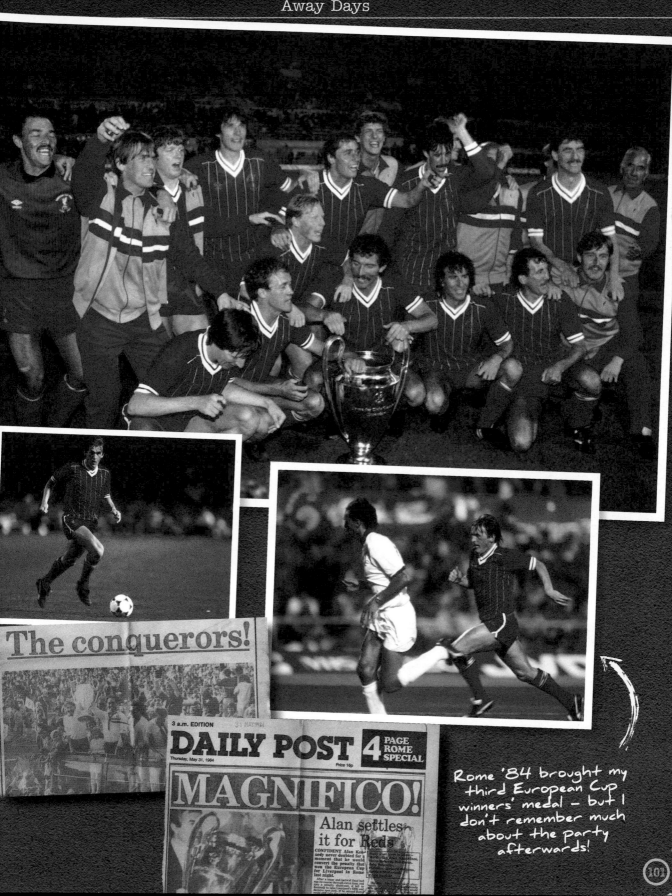

The conquerors!

3 a.m. EDITION   31 MAY 1984

DAILY POST   **4 PAGE ROME SPECIAL**
Thursday, May 31, 1984   Price 16p

MAGNIFICO!

Alan settles it for Reds

CONFIDENT Alan Kennedy only never doubled for a moment that he would convert the penalty that won the European Cup for Liverpool in Rome last night.

After a tense and tactical final but his missionaries throughout time and into a penalty shoot-out, it was a penalty Liverpool's fifth and decisive spot kick. If he missed there would still have...

Rome '84 brought my third European Cup winners' medal – but I don't remember much about the party afterwards!

Talking in my sleep? Don't believe the lads!

I always roomed with Graeme Souness at Liverpool. Before that it was Emlyn Hughes who was on the phone every two minutes.

When I was rooming with Graeme, Terry Mac and Thommo used to come into our room on a Friday night for a bit of banter.

I used to take a sleeping pill so I could get to sleep. They would then be telling me what I'd supposedly said in my sleep even before I went to sleep, but I didn't believe them. They were winding me up.

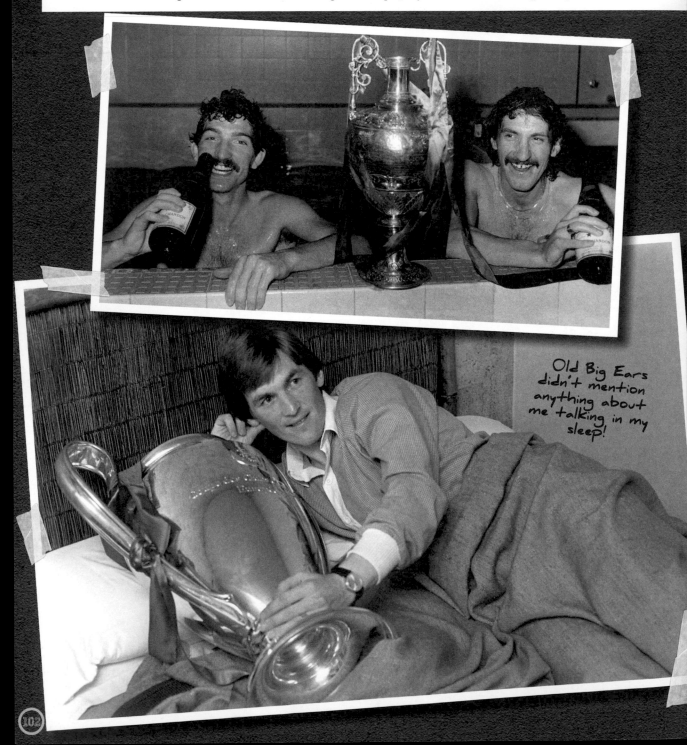

Old Big Ears didn't mention anything about me talking in my sleep!

From cards to iPads

We used to have a card school when we'd be on the road to away games.

It's different now. Players have iPads and iPods now to pass the time while travelling. They might sit next to each other but they don't talk much.

They text each other and get off the coach wearing head phones. I don't think they are listening to motivation tapes! It's just their own music.

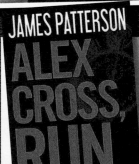

It might not look like it in this picture but we used to interact with each other on the way to games a bit more than current players do

Well red, not well read

I don't mind reading as long as it's big writing with small chapters and there's something happening!

I don't like these books that are too descriptive. James Patterson is an easy read with his suspense and thriller novels.

Group celebrations

The best celebrations in football are when you can celebrate together as a team. Clubs are able to do that far more than international teams.

When you play an international, everybody gets off after the game. You go and see the family and then you start to head home before going back to your clubs.

In the aftermath of matches, even when you qualify for World Cups, it's different to when you've achieved something with your club.

We beat Czechoslovakia 2-1 at Hampden in 1973 to qualify for the World Cup in West Germany, but all the boys couldn't get together to celebrate. They were all thinking about getting back to their clubs.

In reverse, when my Liverpool team beat Cardiff City to win the Carling Cup in 2012 there were internationals the following midweek so there were only three or four of us on the train coming back.

It didn't take anything away from the win, but it was just that the aftermath and the whole atmosphere was different than it could've been.

When you win something, you want to celebrate as a group. You want to enjoy it because there are only two or three opportunities a year.

Finishing fourth in the Premier League and qualifying for Europe is a big thing now, but it's not one of those occasions when you all get together and celebrate.

Winning a cup is special and it was disappointing that, because of circumstances, we couldn't celebrate properly.

We were able to celebrate as a team after clinching the 1983 title

The place I'd love to visit

When it comes to holidays, I just go where Marina tells me to go!

We've been to South Africa. I had never been before. It was fantastic. It seems a long way, but you have a good sleep on the plane, wake up and you're there.

I never found my way to the original Spioenkop hill on that trip, but it is my aim to pay a visit. My daughter Kelly went there during the World Cup, so I am going to go and have a look.

The Spioenkop hill in South Africa

Sorry Marina, the mini belongs to ALL the lads!

Graeme Souness got a music centre for creating the goal that won the European Cup for Liverpool in 1978.

There was a Mini up for grabs for the person who actually scored the goal and with me getting the winner Marina thought we had won a car.

She was all smiles after the game but I said: "Sorry, the two prizes have gone into the kitty – we're using the money for a players' night out."

My goal won the European Cup in 1978, but the Mini I was given went into the team kitty

The Scots take over Liverpool

In 1977 we played Wales at Anfield and won 2-0 to qualify for the World Cup, but we couldn't go anywhere to celebrate.

Everybody went their own way afterwards and I was still living in the Holiday Inn in Liverpool then, being right at the start of my Anfield career.

I couldn't get back into the hotel for Scottish fans! They'd taken over the place.

Winning the cup at Wembley was for Hillsborough families

The most satisfying victory at Wembley was in 1989 when we won the FA Cup, but it was all because of what it stood for after Hillsborough and the solace for families who were still grieving the loss of their loved ones.

For me, that is the most poignant of our cup wins. It's the one that meant the most for many, many reasons, mostly outside football.

Liverpool won a lot of trophies at Wembley and we are grateful for every single one, but that was a special day for us.

We entered the League Cup to win it – just like we did in 1982 against Spurs →

We always gave 100 per cent in every competition

Down the years, I've often smiled when critics have declared that the League Cup is not very important. In recent years they have been claiming that the stature of the FA Cup has diminished.

These competitions only lack importance if you've never won them. The importance comes with how far you get in the tournament.

It's probably easier for some people to get knocked out earlier rather than go close and then get beaten. But for us, we never underestimated anything and always tried to win everything that was in front of us. Fortunately we did, more often than not.

Even the Screen Sport Super Cup that we played in when we were banned from Europe after Heysel was something we wanted to win.

It makes me wonder why, all of a sudden, today's super-fit players are unable to compete for 60 games a year when we were playing 70-odd?

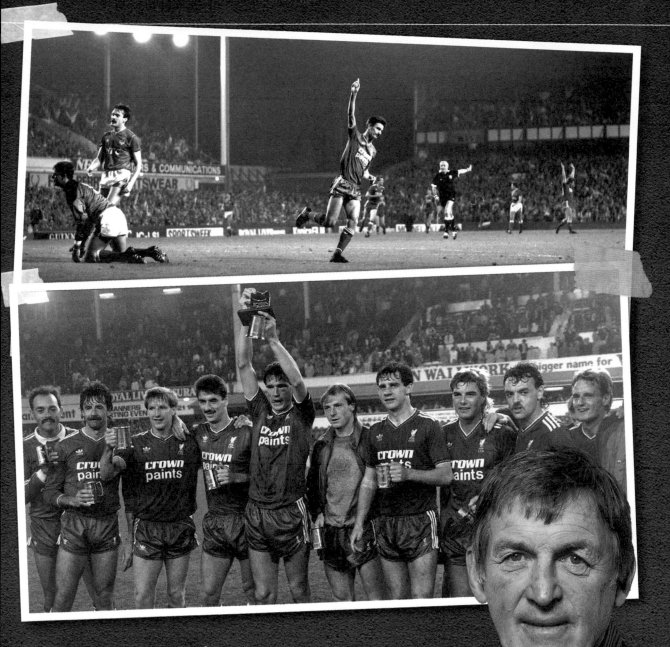

'I've often smiled when critics have declared that the League Cup isn't important. Even the Screen Sport Super Cup was something we wanted to win'

In action against Nottingham Forest, Spurs and West Ham. Whether we won it or not, we always took the League Cup seriously

I just can't get my head around it. If you keep telling someone they're tired, it's a really good excuse not to perform.

Just play. If you're bad, it's because you're bad, not because you're tired. Liverpool just played in every situation when I was there.

The critics kept saying we never trained. It was nonsense. The Boot Room staff knew everything about what had gone on before and they were so up to date, keeping a log day in, day out of everyone who trained and everyone who didn't.

They wrote down injuries that had taken place, why it might have happened and they repeated it and repeated it. Their great intelligence in the preparation of players should never be underestimated. For instance, if you had a persistent injury they would even be checking if you had changed your car.

Someone would need a cartilage operation. They would be straight into their books. What happened? What might have changed to cause it?

The Boot Room staff were well ahead of their time and that was a great help to us. If you prepared properly you would never be as tired as some people suggested you might be.

Tiredness was never a factor when we were beating Everton (top in 1984) and Manchester United (below in 1983) to the League Cup

THE GLORIOUS DOUBLE

So many people must share the credit for an historic season

STEP ONE: THE TITLE

My goal didn't win the title at Stamford Bridge

My goal at Stamford Bridge on May 3, 1986, might have won Liverpool the game at Chelsea in the final match of the season, but it didn't win the championship. That was won over the whole season.

We only got three points for the Chelsea win. You cannot crystallise it into what happened in one game. Ronnie Whelan's goal in the 2-0 win over Leicester was another big one, but it was just part of the effort over the whole season.

You never remember the games where you were lucky, either. You only tend to remember the games where you were unlucky.

People remember the photo of me pointing towards the fans with a smile across my face after I had scored that goal at Stamford Bridge.

The referee shouted "Don't go off the pitch."

I just ran towards the fans with my hands held high and with a smile that said everything about how I felt.

'My goal might have won the Chelsea game in the final match of the season but Ronnie Whelan's goal in the 2-0 win at Leicester was another big one'

✓ QPR (March 86)

✓ Manchester City (March 86)

✓ Tottenham (March 86)

✓ Coventry (April 86)

✓ Birmingham (April 86)

✓ Newcastle (December 85)

'When we beat Everton at Wembley in 1986 it was a landmark moment for Liverpool FC. I will never forget the finale to my first season as player-manager'

STEP TWO: THE CUP

Sharing the Double with Bob

Bob joined the celebrations when we clinched the title in 1986

A win against Everton at Wembley completed the Double

A landmark moment

When we beat Everton at Wembley in 1986 it was a landmark moment for Liverpool FC – our first ever league and FA Cup double.

Of course, I will never forget the finale to my first season as player-manager, but the day was particularly special because old Bob was there to enjoy it.

He didn't want to take any of the credit or the

121

limelight, but we were all so proud that he was with us.

I still can't believe that Bob never achieved a league and FA Cup double in his own right considering all that he won at Liverpool. Everybody still admires him for everything he did.

Bob would do anything for me and it was a wonderful thing to have him around when I was asked to become Liverpool's player-manager in 1985.

He talked to players and gave them advice. For me, it was great that I knew he was there.

He never tried to undermine me. He never tried to take the lead in anything. He always stood back. Bob would come to me and say: "Is it all right if I say this or that?"

I would say: "Bob, you can say whatever you want to the players. You are only going to be helping us."

To have him alongside me when I started out was a great thing, as it was with Ronnie Moran, Roy Evans and Tom Saunders. Bob was special for what he offered.

Our cup run in 1986 saw us get past York City (above) and Southampton

Bob had seen and done it all during my time as a player, so it was great to have his support when I became player-manager

The Anfield ENGINE ROOM

The Liverpool FC dressing room and what made us tick...

Superstitions in the dressing room included what order players were given a rub down in

Before a match we'd all eat chocolate biscuits

If we lost a game I'd hope new clothes would bring better luck

Superstitions and Liverpool's first rotation system

I used to start off the season thinking: 'I'm not going to be superstitious this year,' but I couldn't help it.

I don't know if this is superstition, ritual or whatever the terminology is, but it started on a Friday before we were playing when I was at Liverpool.

We used to go down to Melwood on the bus. I would have to go and get the tea for Warky and Graeme. Then we had chocolate biscuits

and had to take them in the same rotation. We had to sit in the same place when Bob or Joe were taking the team meetings.

You would get up in the morning and shave in a certain way. You would drive to the ground in a certain way.

After that there would be a new shirt for a game to see if it brought luck, but then we would lose a match and I would try a new tie instead. I didn't mind getting new

shirts, ties, underpants or socks in the hope they were lucky, but when it got to buying lucky suits I thought: 'Wait a minute!'

I don't know why we were all superstitious. Maybe it's a comfort zone thing.

It was unbelievable what we used to do. The same people even had to go into the dressing room toilet in rotation! You would find yourself saying: "No, it's his turn."

Mirror, mirror on the wall...what's that all about?

When I signed in 1977, I remember there was a full length mirror just inside the dressing room door. There was an electrical point next to it.

When it's your first day, you don't know what is going on. I kept thinking: 'An electrical point next to a mirror?'

I left it and then the boys started coming in with small holdalls and toilet bags. We never had anything like that at Celtic. All the gear would be lying in the middle of the floor. You were lucky if you got a clean pair of pants! I was saying to myself: 'What's this all about?'

Anyway, we went to training, on the bus in those days, and then came back to Anfield. It was then I discovered what the electric point was for – the hairdryers!

There was all kinds of gel about and aftershave. I thought: 'What's going on here?'

Terry Mac used to have a comb with long prongs because he had a perm. He used to stand in front of the mirror, giving it all that. Terry Mac's haircut...it was as if it had been parted with an axe, straight down the middle. I thought: 'Someone must have a sense of humour in here.'

The dressing room was brilliant. The banter, the wind-ups, there was always something going on.

We had a tight group and while some might have lived in Southport while others lived on the Wirral, there was never a divide. I made my own friends within the team, but everybody was a team-mate. There was never any division.

A great dressing room is hugely important because you spend a lot more time preparing for a game than you do playing. You need to have a sense of humour and you certainly need to have a thick skin.

It's great to get everybody together. The camaraderie in every dressing room I was in was brilliant.

The bus to Anfield went via Warrington, the M62 and the M57

Bruce switches to bizarre ritual

On a Friday, before home matches, we would be taken away to the Lord Daresbury Hotel in Warrington. It would be a quarter-to-eight for a pick-up at Kirkby just outside Liverpool.

We would get on the coach, everybody together. We would go there, get a cup of tea and a piece of toast and watch whatever was on the television at 9pm at night.

Then we'd sleep, get up the following morning and the pre-match get-together would be at 12 o'clock. We would then be back on the bus and straight to the game.

Going up Utting Avenue as we got close to the ground, we would have a guess what the crowd might be and when we got into the dressing room everybody had their own routine.

The rituals would kick in again. Some would put their right boot on first, or their left boot, or their jersey on last. Everyone had their own little routine. There was a rotation about who would be rubbed down first and who would be rubbed last. Everything was laid out.

It would also be clear who would go out onto the pitch first and who would go on last, or whatever.

Every sport has its own idiosyncrasies. If it helped you psychologically as part of your preparation, that was fine. Everybody had their own wee thing to do. Even the chairman used to come in and just say hello to everybody.

Bruce Grobbelaar joined the club a few years after I did and he used to have a warm-up routine using the light switch in the dressing room.

He used to hit the ball at the light switch until he knocked the lights off. We were playing at Plough Lane, the old Wimbledon ground, one year and their manager Bobby Gould came in after the game.

We had won 2-1 and were having a drink when he said: "By the way, I done you there."

"What do you mean?" I said. "The light switch!" he replied. "We put a cover on it. I'd read that it was part of Bruce's routine trying to knock the lights off so I thought it would be a psychological advantage if he couldn't do it."

"Bobby," I said. "It was a waste of time. He only does it at the home games!"

Obviously it didn't work, but that was an example of how an opposing manager would try to do something to upset our pre-match routine.

Following Shankly's routine

When we went away with Liverpool it was very much the same routine that we had for games at Anfield. We had our breakfast in bed and at 12 o'clock it was the pre-match get-together wherever we were staying.

Bob Paisley used to talk about the opposition on a Friday. He talked about us as well and what we had done, or hadn't done, in the previous games.

In his meeting, Bob would use a plastic board that sat on the top of a table in the middle of the floor. Everybody sat in exactly the same seat. Joe Fagan and Ronnie Moran were the same. They had their rituals as well.

Joe and Ronnie had a say in everything that was done. Whether they actually spoke in a particular meeting depended on how the conversation went.

Bob would ask if any of the players had anything to say and Joe and Ronnie would have their opinions. They could speak freely whenever they wanted and although it was mostly Bob who did the team meeting, the contribution Ronnie, Joe and Roy Evans made was huge.

You might wonder what goes on in a dressing room on a matchday, especially at half-time.

At Liverpool, if you needed to be told off, you'd get told off. Players are not immune from criticism, but it was always done in the best interests of the team.

There was nobody in all my time at Liverpool who put

themselves first. The team was always the most important thing.

That's a great credit to the people who were there before I arrived because the club was set in its ways. The players were set in their ways.

Shanks had come in and laid down the dos and don'ts for everybody. He stressed what was right and what was wrong. When you came into the set-up, you followed the routine everyone else was in, so the education came long before I was there. We all just tried to carry it on for the people who came in after us.

When I first arrived, there weren't too many players who would be outspoken or have an opinion other than the staff. Then Graeme Souness arrived! Obviously, Graeme was opinionated – that's why he went on to have success as a manager.

It wouldn't be a one-off that there was an argument in the dressing room that he was involved in.

I was one of those who had an opinion as well, but there was never any animosity or never anything carried over. Speaking out was done for a specific reason and that was to make us better.

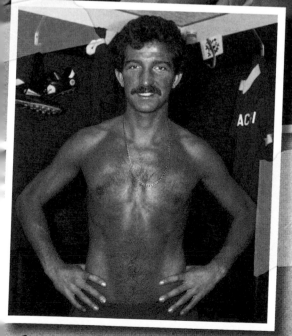

Graeme Souness was opinionated in the dressing room but we all just wanted to make the team better

'Shanks had come in and laid down the dos and don'ts for everybody. We tried to carry it on for the people who came after us'

Preparation over speeches

I was never in the Liverpool dressing room with Shanks but most clubs had a little board with counters that represented the opposition to explain tactical formations and the like.

They famously say that Shanks once swept all the opposing players off the board at West Ham to get a point across. Things would be said, but you didn't always remember it. The preparation had already been done and that was more important than a big speech before a game.

Having said that, Bob was quite good on Friday mornings. He just wanted to know that you would play at the right tempo and that your mind was properly set.

Shanks, Bob, Joe...they were all from the same mould. They knew what they had to do and if you failed to perform properly then you were in trouble.

Shanks, Bob and Joe were all from the same mould

Ronnie Moran oversees a Melwood tactics session over the sort of board Shanks once famously brushed West Ham's players off

Humble, respectful and appreciative

All the managers I worked under
wanted to win and prepare the
best way they could. To them, it
was important what you did at
the training ground.

It was important to know what
you wanted to get from a training
session. It was also important
what the players did away from
the training ground.

If we didn't prepare properly
away from the training ground,

we are all going to be in trouble.

People like big Jock, Bob and
Joe never ever sought publicity
for themselves. It was part of the
whole ethos. The humility that
they showed throughout their
success was unbelievable and an
example to everybody.

Some managers come in, win
three games in a row and all of
a sudden they think they are the
best in the world. These guys

were doing it for years. They
were humble, respectful and
appreciative of what other people
did for them.

They never thought they had
done anything themselves and
they were always quick, ready
and willing to pay tribute and
compliments to other people.
That was the mark of them as
people and also a mark of why
they were so successful.

Plank of the Year - an award nobody wanted

At Liverpool we used to have our very own players' awards night and I always hoped I wouldn't be the one on the receiving end of some of the 'awards'. You had to stand up for yourself.

The one that caused most hilarity was called 'Plank of the Year'. We used to present that one at the Christmas party and we had three separate categories: Young Plank of the Year, Up and Coming Plank of the Year and Plank of the Year.

There was also the 'Player of the Month' award and if you won that you got a case of vodka! Imagine trying to do that now! It would be all over the papers.

No-one ever kept it. We used to give the vodka to Jack Ferguson, the manager of the old Holiday Inn, and he would replace it with champagne and store

it up for us until we went to the Christmas party. Not everyone drank vodka, but they would have a go at the champagne.

I have to say that I never won Plank of the Year – the competition was too fierce! It was the same runners and riders every year.

In no particular order there would be Bruce Grobbelaar and Stevie Nicol. Rushie denies it, but he would always be there. Ronnie Whelan would be another one who would dispute it. Paul

Walsh was a contender when he came.

If you made a mistake when you were trying to say something, that was it. You were accumulating points for December time.

There was no trophy – we didn't actually hand over a plank! – but the winners were never allowed to forget it.

That was better than a medal. It was just something stupid that carried on and gained momentum. It brought everyone together.

One of Rushie's many hat-trick match balls shows evidence of him being one of the 'planks'

Some of our contenders for 'Plank of the Year' pictured having a laugh not long after I'd left the club

Driving Stevie mad

The lads were looking to have a laugh at every opportunity.

I remember when we – me, Big Al, Graeme and Chico, our nickname for Steve Nicol – were in the car on the motorway going up to Scotland and it had been snowing.

Stevie was asked to get out and wipe the windscreen because we couldn't see. As soon as he got out, we drove off. He only had a t-shirt on!

Every time he caught up we would drive away again. It was unbelievable.

My Anfield MANAGERS

136

Bob's office door was always open

Outside of the games, Bob Paisley's door was always open. It was the same with Joe Fagan when he took over.

You can't have a closed door and try and run a successful football club. You have got to have communication, discussion and dialogue with people so Bob's door was always open for people to go in and speak to him.

He was really unassuming, but unbelievable at making the correct decisions. No one knew how he came to that decision or the rationale he used, but he knew. He was just brilliant at getting decisions right. In management, the more you get right, the more chance you have of being successful.

He would tell you something about the opposition if it was relevant. He would use the press to get a message out there about the opposition that might be helpful to us.

He never undermined anybody in the press who was on his side and he was always really supportive of people who were representing the football club. Everybody knew exactly where they stood.

Bob was courageous at making decisions and there were a lot he had to make with regards to picking teams. There was one season when we only used 15 players or something and won the league. That is unbelievable. It must have been hard for the rest of the lads who couldn't get a game, but it was amazing for so few players to be used to win a championship.

Everything he did was in the best interests of the football club. He never thought of himself. That reflects how the football club was and how it should always be.

People remember him switching a traditional centre-forward like Ray Kennedy into a top class midfielder, but there were hundreds of decisions he made, probably thousands.

He had this ability to judge the strengths of players and how they might fit in. He signed me, Alan Kennedy, Alan Hansen. He signed Graeme Souness, Rushie, and Ronnie Whelan.

He signed Phil Neal and Terry Mac. He brought in a lot of really good players and they all just came in and fitted into that dressing room because of what had been put in place before.

When you arrived at Liverpool, other people showed you the ropes. We tried to do the same for those who came in after us.

I don't think there has ever been a football team that has been successful without a good dressing room. I've never been in a Liverpool dressing room that has been selfish.

Bob also had this remarkable knack of spotting and understanding injuries. Someone would be walking across the pitch and he would say 'he's got a cartilage problem'. The guy would only be strolling across the pitch!

But that's what he started his backroom life as after being a very good player. He began as a physio, or trainer as it was then. He just had an unbelievable eye for picking out an injury.

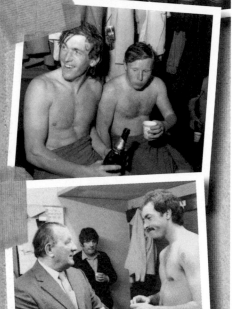

Every kid's favourite uncle

It was brilliant for old Bob the way it ended for him at Liverpool ahead of Joe coming in.

We won the Milk Cup in 1983 after beating Manchester United at Wembley. Graeme came in and said: "Why don't we let Bob go up for the trophy?"

It was unheard of then for a manager to receive the trophy. Everybody went 'Yeah, that's brilliant.'

Bob went up the Wembley steps with one bit of a scarf over his front and the other over his back. It just summed him up. He was more interested in what he was going up to receive than how he looked going up there.

He picked up the trophy and we won the championship that season as well. So it was brilliant for him to go out on such a wonderful note.

I don't think Bob ever changed. He used to get up in the morning, leave the house, stop off at a garage in Prescot Road and go in the back where they had a tea room, have a cup of tea, pick out his horses, get back in the car and go to Anfield.

He'd be in his office, go to training, come back and do what he had to do, and that was his day.

Bob would prepare us to play in the matches. He was really humble and we appreciated it and what he did. He won three European Cups and must have been really proud and excited about what he had achieved, but he was just like Uncle Bob, every kid's favourite uncle.

He was brilliant with people. Brilliant in football and brilliant making decisions – a really welcoming and humble guy.

Yes, he was also tough, but it's tough to be a manager. It's even more difficult if you shirk away from the tough decisions. You can make life more difficult for yourself.

If it's right, it's right. You've got to go and do it, and he did. That's why he was so successful.

Graeme Souness suggested Bob collected the Milk Cup when we won it in 1983 and everyone thought it was a great idea

Business as usual under Joe Fagan

Bob decided he wanted to retire in 1983 and Joe was coming in to replace him which was great for everyone in the dressing room.

We all knew Joe and that he would act a little bit differently than he had as Bob's right-hand man.

Ronnie would move up and Roy Evans would come in so it was great for us. Joe was a friendly face, a seamless change. We knew old Bob would be missed, but Joe was coming in.

Like Bob, when he was offered the manager's job, he might have been a little reluctant to take it, but he took it because the club was more important than anything else.

He won three trophies in his first year. That was fantastic.

Joe didn't say much. He didn't lose his temper much, so when he did shout you knew you were in trouble. There was nothing wrong with that.

He didn't actually create a problem. It was the person he was shouting at who caused the problem.

'Joe didn't say much so when he did shout you knew you were in trouble'

Putting Liverpool first...with a great supporting team

The most important thing to come from Bob and Joe was the fact that the football club is more important than any individual.

You have to make decisions. You have to make the correct decisions. You are entrusted to make decisions. At a football club you are representing everybody – the players, the fans, the owners. You cannot shirk away from your responsibilities.

You won't get success just because you are there. You get success because everybody shares in it and can do their own job. If none of those things happen then there will be a problem.

When I stepped forward to become manager, Bob stepped forward to help me. It was like it was my birthday. I had the most successful manager in British football upstairs to call upon.

If I needed a conversation, he was there to listen. He was really educated in football as well as life, a fantastic person to bounce things off. I also had Ronnie Moran, Roy Evans and Tom Saunders to work with. I even had Tom's desk moved into my office. If I couldn't be successful with those people around me there was only one person to blame.

They were always with me. They would always be taken into the conversations of the games that were coming up, the people you wanted to buy, what you wanted to do.

We would discuss things on a Friday night, most often in my room. Then once it was decided or I had made a decision about the team we were going with or whatever, they were 100% behind me.

There were no rifts. Not even the slightest hint of them having a slightly different view. If you said you wanted to do something or try something, they were with you all the way.

You can't ask for more than that.

PAISLEY'S TRIBUTE TO 'KING' KENNY

'He's unique, he thinks soccer 24 hours a day'

By GRAHAM CLARK

Y DALGLISH was
involved in his first
business since be-
g manager of Liver-

newest and youngest
First Division boss
ding transfer talks with
am's Paul Allen with a
a £600,000 deal.
while Dalglish launched
t into his new, some-
nexpected role, the man
ll partner him as
of the Merseyside club
nthusiastic about the set-

WISE

Paisley, the wise old owl
field, has lined up along-
e Scottish international
e Liverpool into a new

on't THINK the partner-
ill work, I KNOW it

the 46-year-old former
ld Manager, now of-
y described as team
tant, went on to sing
sh's praises.
nny is different. In fact
nique. He thinks football
urs a day.

"I see Kenny and I discuss-
ing things in much the same
way I did with Bill Shankly.
We might not agree all the
time but he will have the final
say and there will be no
animosity afterwards," said
Paisley.

Dalglish, for his part, is
already on record as saying he
will rely heavily on Paisley as
well, indeed, as his prede-
cessor Joe Fagan and the rest
of the Anfield backroom staff.

SUPPORT

"They and the board have
given me their full support and
I am sure Mr Paisley's vast
experience will help me to
have a successful managerial
career," said Kenny.

That career has already be-
gun with a vengeance, for as
well as spearheading a club in
turmoil following the trauma
of Brussels, Dalglish is turning
his thoughts to the playing side
of the game he will continue to
grace next season.

Talks with Allen today about
a move to Anfield will be followed by discussions with Ian
Rush and Craig Johnston,
players who were team-mates
in the European Cup Final on
Wednesday.

Bot have been consistently
linked with moves — the
striker to Italy and the mid-
field man to Chealsea — and
Dalglish now wants to know
exactly where they stand.

It's a historic start to an
awesome challenge for one of
Scotland's favourite football
sons.

KENNY DALGLISH. Having £600,0
transfer talks

7

IN THE
HOTSEAT

The transition from being just one of the lads to being the boss was a fine balancing act, but, fortunately, my step into management brought more success

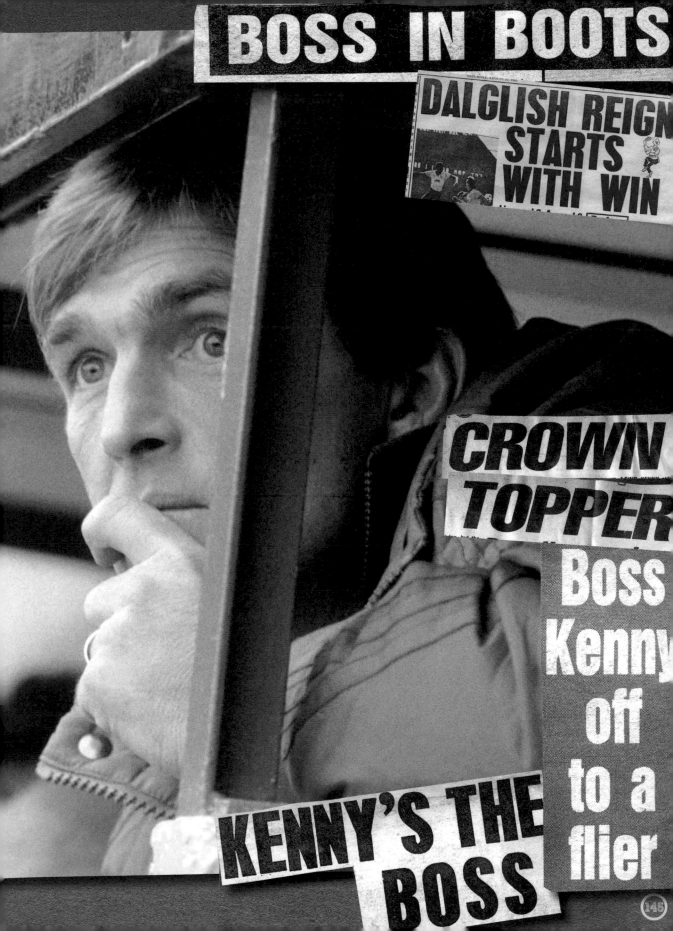

BOSS IN BOOTS

DALGLISH REIGN STARTS WITH WIN

CROWN TOPPER

Boss Kenny off to a flier

KENNY'S THE BOSS

145

I don't know why they asked me to manage Liverpool

The year before I got the manager's job, I signed a contract for another four years. The club offered me four years at 33 years of age. I asked Peter Robinson 'why?'

He said: "I just think you deserve it." I said: "Peter, it's a bad deal for you. I'm not 23, I'm 33."

"I know what age you are," he said, "but we are delighted to offer you the contract."

"Give me the pen," I said.

The following year I got a phone call when Joe announced he was leaving. It was Peter. "The chairman would like to come and speak to you at home," he said, "we would like to offer you the manager's job." He arranged to come round on the Sunday.

I phoned up my dad and Marina's dad. They both said 'I think you are capable of doing it. You've got to have a go,' but I still wanted to keep playing. Obviously, the danger for me was trying to do two jobs.

Why they chose to ask me I don't know. I just know it was a great honour. At the meeting I said to them: "I'll try it, but if I'm no good, I'll just go back to playing."

We started from there.

Peter Robinson

KENNY'S CHANCE

By CHICK YOUNG

SCOTLAND'S most famous football son is 24 hours from making another astonishing piece of sporting history.

Kenneth Mathieson Dalglish M.B.E. will be named the new manager of Liverpool at the age of 34 in succession to Joe Fagan who has quit because — as he says — "I'm too old and tired. It is a job for a younger man."

It is a huge gamble by the Merseyside club for such as John Greig at Rangers found that stepping from the playing ranks to the manager's chair is a promotion plagued with problems.

But if anyone can succeed then it is Dalglish. For just about everything he has touched has turned Midas-style to soccer gold.

He has won more Scottish caps than any other player — 98 — and only Denis Law has scored as many goals for our country — 30. He won every domestic trophy with Celtic and in England only the FA Cup has eluded him with Liverpool.

But the compensation for that has come in the shape of three

Dalglish set to step up as manager

European Cup winning medals and a reputation as one of the greatest players in the world.

He will command instant respect as boss of the Anfield club, although he will continue to play — an arrangement which will please Jock Stein because it means that Dalglish will remain an integral part of Scotland's World Cup plans.

GUIDE

And it looks as if Liverpool will tempt former boss Bob Paisley to come out of retirement to guide Dalglish father-figure style.

Today Dalglish, who moved from Celtic to Merseyside in a £440,000 deal in 1977, was on his way back to Liverpool with his team-mates only too aware that even the sensational

news of his step-up is dwarfed by the horrors of Brussels last night.

But, in any case, there would be no boasts from the man who is still a proud Glaswegian.

For despite being the biggest idol in British football and on the threshold of his fourth World Cup finals, he has always gone about his business modestly.

Dalglish signed a new four-year contract a year ago — at the age of 33.

OPINION

And that started the rumours that he was being groomed as the club's new manager in a dynasty which has seen only three names in a quarter of a century . . . Bill Shankly, Bob Paisley and Joe Fagan.

Before that deal was signed speculation was rife that Dalglish was on the way out at Anfield — and that the last days of his career would be spent with Rangers.

Dalglish said: "People were entitled to say that I was at the end of my international career after the 1982 World Cup but it didn't matter to me what they think or what I think even.

KENNY DALGLISH
— the Midas touch

KENNY'S THE BOSS

The lads were waiting for me to make a mistake

I remember my first meeting at Melwood as player-manager.

I knew what the lads were like because I had been part of that group. I knew the players would be sitting there, watching, listening and waiting for me to make a mistake.

I knew they would pick on anything instantly. I said: "If you think it's funny, you come and stand on this side. You try and say a few words. It's not easy, by the way."

Two months earlier I had been with them, sitting and listening to what Joe was saying. Players always pick up on things. It's part of the dressing room spirit.

I suppose leaving the group spirit, getting away from the dressing room banter was the hardest part for me. I loved being part of everything that went on in there, the laughter, the banter and the jokes.

I have to say the lads quickly accepted the change. They were brilliant and really supportive.

The players were sitting there and their future was suddenly being directed by someone who had no experience whatsoever of being a manager. To their credit, they were fully supportive.

I'LL SETTLE for the kind of start today that we had in the first derby game of the season, when we were a goal up at Goodison Park after exactly one minute, and I'm not saying that just because I was the man who scored it.

Having caught Everton cold, we found ourselves two goals ahead with just over a quarter of an hour gone, and by half-time we had made it 3-0, with Steve McMahon scoring against his old club.

The second half followed a somewhat different pattern, though, because Everton narrowed the gap soon after the restart, and although they didn't get a second until close to time, we were unable to get another goal and the final scoreline was made to look much closer, at 3-2.

I reckon the crowd of more than 51,500 had their money's worth that Saturday afternoon back in September, when the sun was still shining and the mud and snow were still to come. We've seen a few changes in the weather since then.

In those early days, with only nine matches gone, Manchester United were leading it at the top and Liverpool were second, though trailing by nine points, while Everton were down in sixth place and 11 points behind United.

Everton showed against us that they were ready to keep on fighting, and they showed during the months that followed that they have this quality of resilience, for after trailing United by 17 points at one stage, they not only closed the gap, but became the first club to overtake them.

Now comes the return derby game, and once again it's going to be a battle right through the 90 minutes. It's always a battle, anyway, but with both of us still in contention for the title, the points are of special significance. I just hope the outcome is the same as last time – even if there's only one goal in it again.

Dropping Kenny Dalglish

I was reluctant to pick myself at the beginning of my time as manager.

Paul Walsh **(below)** had made a great start for us but then he got injured in the January and I came back in.

I hadn't played too many times and it was more difficult to name myself as substitute because you get so caught up in the game when you're the manager. It takes so much out of you watching from the sidelines that you might as well be playing.

As a sub, you find yourself under pressure to go on because you have been through the mill for the previous 60 to 70 minutes, so I stopped making myself sub because I didn't think it was fair on anybody.

But there wasn't much difference when I was player-manager. If I was getting ready to play, Bob, Ronnie and Roy would have a bit more to say around the dressing room, but nothing they said was ever against anything I wanted to do.

They were really fabulous in those situations.

"It was more difficult to name myself as substitute because you get so caught up in the game when you're the manager"

Managerial pointers from Bob

I didn't know what to expect when I went in during the close season in 1985 with things about to change. I got the manager's job in the May after the Heysel Disaster.

I went in and Bob was already in. I was sitting in the same office that he had occupied throughout his career. Joe had also used that office and now I was in there.

Bob was sitting on the other side of the desk and I just said: "What do I do now?"

He said: "Well, the phone might ring." I said: "We've got a phone in the house. If anybody wants to ring me, they can get me just as easily at home."

Bob said: "No, you've got to be here, just in case." That was him telling me that my circumstances had changed and that I was a manager now with more responsibility than just looking after myself.

It was true. I'm not saying the changeover was totally smooth, but if you are going to do a player-manager's job at 34 years of age, the best help you could ever get would be from within the football club I was in. I could not have had a better chance to become successful.

Winning the League and FA Cup double in that first year was beyond anyone's expectations.

I wasn't sure if I was going to be any good, but I was determined to try my best. To walk away with a double at the end of it was not because I was that good, but because of the whole infrastructure of the club.

The players were fantastic, so were the staff and everyone upstairs. Of course, the fans were right behind us too. It was beyond my wildest dreams to be part of all of that.

YOU'LL NEVER WALK ALONE

SCOTLAND'S greatest sporting son, Kenny Dalglish, has made football history again.

At the age of 34 he has become player-manager of one of the most famous clubs in the world and so has accepted an awesome task.

Sports Times went to the heart of Anfield to talk to Kenny in his new office about his hopes and dreams for the future and he spoke frankly about the job he has taken on.

The Kenny Dalglish interview is the big one . . . and as usual, you read it first in the Times.

EXCLUSIVE BY CHICK YOUNG

THE early days of Kenny Dalglish as manager of Liverpool Football Club are plagued with a problem.

What Kenneth Mathieson Dalglish, MBE, needs, if the legend is to grow even further, is a coaching course from British Telecom.

The complex of telephones on his desk at Anfield are proving hot to handle for the football immortal who, until his astonishing appointment this summer, probably never realised that 4-2-4 could also be a dialling code.

But Scotland's greatest soccer son will surely score again at his new job and a desk which is nothing short of awesome.

SPECIAL

Dalglish, you see, is backed by a special task force which includes the legendary Bob Paisley. The anthem of the Kop never did ring more true, Kenny, you'll never walk alone.

Dalglish's appointment at 34 as player-manager of Liverpool, the magnitude of it all was drama and the Cup...

It is only now, as the new season dawns, that football is beginning to awaken to that has happened to the Shankly-Paisley-Fagan dynasty.

Kenny Dalglish's new job is marginally easier that solving the national debt.

And he knows it. But he shoulders the responsibility with the same calm, logical, no-promises approach which has made him arguably the most famous British player in history.

His office is deep in the heart of Anfield, at the end of the corridor of the players' lounge, and, frankly, if you were looking for adjectives to describe it you wouldn't use plushy, huge, or elegant.

DISGRACEFUL

But it is from within these walls that Bill Shankly, Bob Paisley, and Joe Fagan built the legend of Liverpool and carved out a reputation of international renown which in world terms only Real Madrid could match.

Now Dalglish, still playing and chasing an international future, must carry this on. And in the wake of the disgraceful happenings in the club.

The Heysel Stadium without an immediate

European future for the first season in decades. It also saw Fagan quit with a sour taste in his mouth from the game which had given him the sweetest moments in his life.

Kenny is in the middle of tremendous pressure. But he is ready for the challenge.

In his office, where the walls are decorated with schoolkids' paintings of the Liverpool players, he spoke openly and frankly of the days ahead.

GREATNESS

"No one needs to tell me what it's all about," he said. "But I didn't hesitate for one second when I was offered the job.

"Look around you and you can feel the greatness of Liverpool Football Club. It is an honour that people in power think I can carry on.

"But I will not go into the new season setting targets or thinking that one trophy win come next May would be enough.

"Never as a player have I eyed a certain number of caps or goals. That is not my style. I will give the job my all and we'll see what happens.

"And neither is it any easier because we didn't have such a wonderful season — by our own

Never underestimate what we've got on Merseyside

One of my biggest memories of the 1986 FA Cup Final at Wembley was of the dads taking their two sons to the match, one in red and white and the other in blue and white. That was something the city of Liverpool should always be proud of. Before the game both sets of supporters were all chanting 'Merseyside, Merseyside'.

I don't think we should ever underestimate what we have got here. Sometimes it is, and sometimes it's not, as good as it was before, but it's still very special to have two teams so vehemently supported in the city of Liverpool who can still go away together and have a drink, a chat and a laugh.

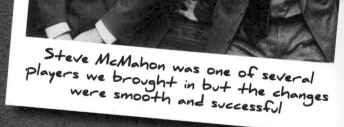

Steve McMahon was one of several players we brought in but the changes were smooth and successful

Seamless change

At the end of my first season as manager I was just delighted for everybody at Anfield. I suppose it looked as if there had been a seamless change.

We had brought Steve McMahon in that season. Liverpool had already bought Jan Molby for the middle of the pitch, Craig Johnston was playing and we had Paul Walsh up front instead of me. We were making six or seven changes.

The fact that it appeared to be a seamless transformation was to do with the players. The new ones slotted in, the existing ones accepted them and everyone was working for each other.

It sounds like we made wholesale changes but it was done in the correct way. The only disappointment for me was that we couldn't get everyone who had made a contribution out on the pitch at Wembley as we completed the double.

Everyone in the dressing room had made a contribution. The supporters had stood by us all the way and kept the belief going. Everybody can be proud of any success – you've only got a problem if you think it's down to one person.

Tom the teacher

I think Tom Saunders was one of the city's youngest headmasters when he got his first senior job in education. He had made a huge success of the Liverpool Boys team and the club recognised his quality, taking him on as youth development officer.

In this role he took over the recruitment side of the younger players, but was also known as our European scout, looking at the opposition for up and coming European games.

It wasn't like nowadays when it is one stop to most destinations. It would be four or five flights for old Tom. He used to travel all over Europe and come back with his reports. He would also go and watch teams here.

When I first became manager, I used to take him in my car on scouting missions. He had to teach me how to watch a game when you are

working, which is very different to watching a match at home on TV. He was fantastic for me, but most importantly for Liverpool. Tom had the total respect of everyone at the club for his wisdom and sound advice.

He was part of a very special set-up. I was very lucky to be part of one of the greatest periods in the club's history.

Sergeant Major Moran and Roy through the ranks

Ronnie Moran was at Liverpool as a player when Bill Shankly first came in. Then he was taken on the backroom staff. Liverpool had a knack of doing that.

The same would eventually happen to Roy Evans. He was told he wouldn't make a regular first-team player, but was asked if he would like to join the backroom team. What a statement that was to someone who was just 23 years of age. Roy took to it like a duck to water and won a record nine Central League Championships in eleven years with the reserves. It was a great record.

Then, when Bob came in, there was Joe and Ronnie. Roy just followed up through the ranks to eventually become manager himself.

Of course, Ronnie had been there for a long time, first playing, then coaching the kids and moving up behind the scenes. He could have a bit of a temper, but it's never a bad thing if you have got someone who is prepared to tell the truth.

They would all get together in the Boot Room after every game. It was a little sanctuary for them. They would never say anything bad about the opposition. They were so clever. Opposing managers thought they were getting an education going in there, but they were being quizzed for information about their own young players, their strengths and weaknesses and what they were like as individuals.

The staff never spoke to anyone in there without trying to extract information from them. It was brilliant.

The Boot Room was on the main dressing room corridor, right next to the drying room. The apprentices used to go in there to clean the boots. The staff would sit in their own little area at the back. There would be Ronnie, Joe, and Roy. Tom Saunders would have his own little chair in the corner where he would sit and have a wee whisky.

The room only had a couple of skips in there and a metal shelf, some pegs to hang up the boots, and more importantly a couple of cupboards to keep the drinks in.

The players very rarely went in. They would shout from outside if they wanted to say something to Ronnie or Joe. If you were invited in, it was brilliant. It was their own little private space during the week when we used to change at Anfield and then take the coach to Melwood.

It was a real privilege for anyone who was asked to step into the Boot Room.

The great **1978/79** team

The great **1987/88** team

GREAT TEAMS FROM DIFFERENT ERAS

How do you choose between two brilliant sides?

Every time you thought it couldn't get any better, another group would come along and set new standards. In 1978/79 we won the championship, conceding just 16 goals. I think we scored 85 goals that same season. You are never going to be unsuccessful if you can turn in stats like that.

Everybody has got their own favourite teams and eras, but for me it was just an honour to play for the club and then to be asked to be manager.

People mention the 1987/88 season, some commentator even suggested that team was

⋮

better than the Brazilians. I wasn't playing then – that's probably why!

We beat Nottingham Forest 5-0 and the legendary Tom Finney watched us and said it was the best performance he had ever seen.

That team was fantastic. Peter Beardsley, John Aldridge, John Barnes, Ray Houghton, Steve McMahon, Ronnie Whelan – top quality in every position. Alan Hansen, Gary Gillespie, Steve Nicol, Barry Venison...it was just fantastic to watch them play and see their movement.

It was about individual ability within a team framework and the training we did, not least the five-a-sides. It was what you got out of those small-sided games and how it was constructed that was important. And it wasn't just that. There were always conditions applied to the training that were pertinent to the way we wanted to play.

That was a great credit to the staff. The message was coming over, but you didn't necessarily realise that you were actually being coached. It was just a joy to be in training.

The great 1987/88 team

Standing together after Hillsborough

The period around Hillsborough was difficult for everyone at the club, but it doesn't compare with the impact on the people who lost loved ones at Hillsborough.

The relatives, the mothers and fathers, the sisters and brothers... they are the ones who suffered more than anyone else.

At that time it was crucial that the club responded in the right way and it was Peter Robinson's wisdom that came into play when we opened the ground up as a point of remembrance for those who had lost their lives. Everybody came together and it was correct that we then became a support for our fans because they had supported us.

It was right that we tried our best to help them in their time of need. The players and the football club were unbelievable. The football world was unbelievably supportive as well. People who had never set foot in Anfield because of intense rivalry now came to pay their respects and share in the grief of the Hillsborough families.

We could not begin to understand how it must have felt for those directly affected by what had happened. We just got on and tried to do whatever we could.

I think the families appreciated the effort the club put in to try and help them. It was a reflection and a sign of the gratitude that we had for them that we stood together to try and help.

The whole process and the campaign to secure justice for the 96 is still in progress, but there is finally light at the end of the tunnel. The families have been unbelievably patient and respectful. They have done everything right. Nobody can have anything but respect for what they have done and how they have handled themselves in the time that they have had to wait.

Any satisfaction or success they might get from any judgments coming forward will be thoroughly deserved because they have been unbelievably focused on bringing out the truth.

People ask me if Hillsborough took its toll personally, but as an individual it's not really important what happened to me. We did what we had to do and I would do exactly the same thing if it was ever to happen again, although I hope it never will.

It's the way you were brought up. It's about a football club that has always been in touch with its supporters. I am still in touch with some of the families and will continue to try and help as much as I possibly can.

Getting back on the pitch again

There has always been a fantastic relationship between Celtic and Liverpool. I don't know where the roots of it originated, but my recollection was that Jock Stein and Bill Shankly were really close.

Jock also had a fantastic friendship with Bill's brother Bob who had a few managers' jobs in Scotland. There was always a close bond.

After the Hillsborough Disaster, Celtic came on the phone and said 'Let us know when you are ready to play a game because we would love to play and remember the Liverpool fans who lost their lives'.

So after we made the decision that the families wanted to go ahead with the rearranged semi-final against Nottingham Forest, we decided to play a game at Celtic Park on April 30, just over two weeks after the disaster. It was an unbelievable sight.

Celtic had played at Morton on the Saturday and then we went up to Celtic Park to play in front of 60,000 people. There were red and white and green and white scarves everywhere and banners right around the track.

The various supporters clubs were there, mixing the red with the green, and the players came out and made a circle as the fans joined together to sing 'You'll Never Walk Alone'. It was unbelievable.

It was fantastic of Celtic to offer their facilities and their team. As an occasion it was truly memorable, possibly for the wrong reasons, but truly remarkable.

LIVERPOOL FC SEASON-BY-SEASON APPEARANCES & GOALS							
Season	Lg	FA	LC	Euro	Other	Total	Goals
1977-78	42	1	9	9	1	62	31
1978-79	42	7	1	4	0	54	25
1979-80	42	8	7	2	1	60	23
1980-81	34	2	8	9	1	54	18
1981-82	42	3	10	6	1	62	22
1982-83	42	3	7	5	1	58	20
1983-84	33	0	8	9	1	51	12
1984-85	36	7	1	7	2	53	6
1985-86	21	6	2	0	2	31	7
1986-87	18	0	5	0	2	25	8
1987-88	2	0	0	0	0	2	0
1988-89	0	0	1	0	1	2	0
1989-90	1	0	0	0	0	1	0
Total	355	37	59	51	13	515	172

No regrets at retiring

I don't remember too much about the day I played my last game for Liverpool in May 1990. It was the night we were presented with the championship. I know we beat Derby County 1-0 and that Gary Gillespie scored, but that's about it.

To win any trophy is hugely rewarding. The last one you win is always the most important.

We were never allowed to rest on our laurels at Liverpool Football Club. Yes, I was retiring as a player, but at 39 that wasn't too bad was it?

I did play at Anfield again that year. I had my testimonial game against Real Sociedad in August 1990 and over 30,000 attended. We won 3-0, but I never scored. If I'd hung up my boots the year before, I might have done!

It was fantastic that so many people came along and it's great that you have an opportunity to say thanks to them, but that was me finished as a player.

It was an emotional day, but how can you have any regrets when you have had the privilege of playing for Liverpool and Celtic?

I was a lucky boy to have played for two of Britain's most successful football clubs.

OPPONENTS FACED MOST OFTEN

28	ARSENAL
25	NOTTINGHAM FOREST
24	MANCHESTER UNITED
23	EVERTON
20	IPSWICH TOWN

I SCORED MOST GOALS AGAINST

11 MANCHESTER CITY
10 IPSWICH TOWN
8 ARSENAL
8 TOTTENHAM
8 WEST BROM

GOODBYE: Dalglish salutes the fans

picture by John Davids

Dalglish dazzles for the last time

KENNY Dalglish rolled back the years as he paid his final playing farewell to Anfield last night.

Two moments of typical Dalglish magic created first half goals for Ian Rush and Steve McMahon in his testimonial match.

Rush added another in the second half as Liverpool cruised to a comfortable victory in front of 30,461 delighted fans who turned

| Liverpool .... 3 |
| Real Sociedad .. 1 |
| by Philip McNulty |

boss Dalglish arou £150,000.

He played for 74 minu putting the ball into the just seconds before his f departure from the Anf stage, only for his effort t ruled out for offside b linesman.

He left to a stand ovation, handing his fam red number seven shirt fan in the handicapp section of Anfield's n stand.

Dalglish addressed fans through a microph and said: "I would like thank each and every on you for the support you b

I'VE SCORED

118 GOALS IN LEAGUE
27 GOALS IN LEAGUE CUP
13 GOALS IN FA CUP
10 GOALS IN EUROPEAN CUP
2 GOALS IN SCREEN SPORT
SUPER CUP
1 GOAL IN EUROPEAN SUPER CUP
1 GOAL IN CHARITY SHIELD

Hanging up my boots at my testimonial against Real Sociedad

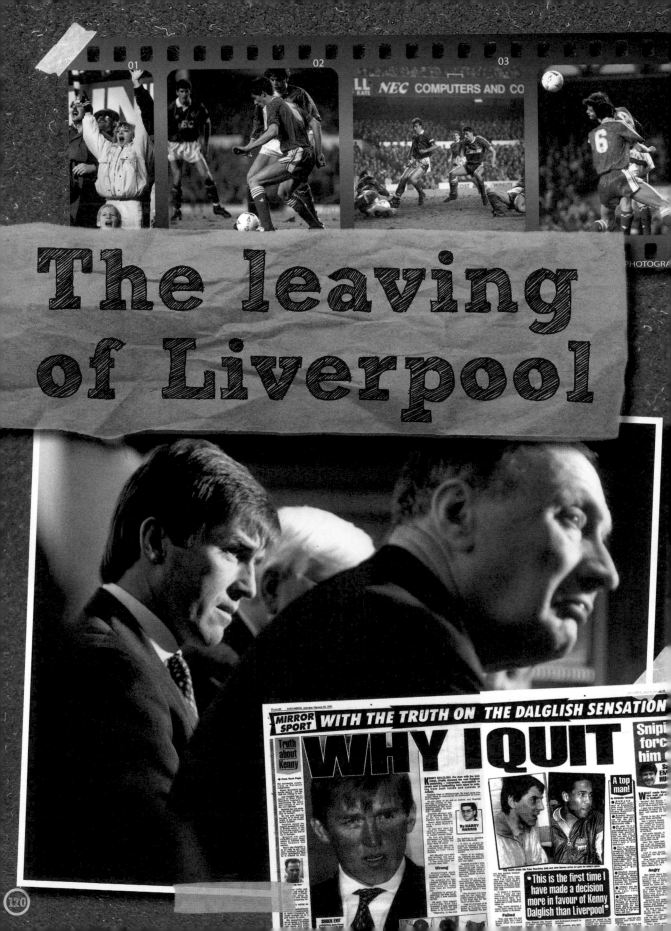

The leaving
of Liverpool

DAILY POST

THE FAC

Reds manager t
all to the Daily P

Saturday, February 23, 1991   Britain's fastest-growing regional daily newspaper   Price 24p

Arnie's money
muscle   Page 21

ock 'n' Roller
Your uncle Page 29

REDS' CHIEF
WHY I QUIT

Plan your weekend here The best guide to what's on arou
Merseyside starts Page 33

Liverpool ECHO

WIRRA
EDITION

KENNY
QUITS

**Anfield boss
sensation!**

Iraq claims ground
war has started

Heseltine rules out
special aid for city

STILL
UNBEATABLE
IN 1991
VOLKSWAGEN
TOM

OTS IMAGES PHOTOGRAPHY PHOTOS SHOOTS IMAGES

Leaving Liverpool in 1991 wasn't a pleasant experience for me. It was the first time that I had made any decision that was more important to Kenny Dalglish than it was to Liverpool Football Club.

For me to go was the right thing to do. If you are in charge and you can't make decisions, or you are taking time to make decisions, or you are unsure if they are right then you don't deserve to be there. The football club doesn't deserve that.

It was right for everybody. While it wasn't good news for me, it had to be done.

The club suggested a sabbatical. I said: "How can it be a sabbatical when I am not coming back?"

You either make a break or you don't make a break. I just could not see how that might have worked. It was best just to cut the cord and go. There was no other answer for me.

I actually decided before the 4-4 FA Cup draw against Everton at Goodison Park that I was going to do it. Even hanging on for a week or two weeks would not have been right. It would've leaked out to the press and everyone would have been under pressure.

It was the right thing to do it there and then because it had been running through my mind.

I had been hesitant to sign a new contract at the start of that season because I felt almost the same then, and that was after we won the title.

During the summer I got a bit of refreshment and then you got back into it, but as the season went on it was more apparent that the decision I had pondered on earlier was the right one and so I had to go.

I wasn't putting any more pressure on myself than I had done in years gone by. You have got to remember that I started playing professional football at 17. That was a long innings. As a player, you only get a few weeks off. You are continually under pressure.

I played for two great clubs. While that was always thoroughly enjoyable, it still brings pressure. I was always working, latterly as a manager.

When does your phone not ring when you are a manager? Even when you go on holiday you are still working. It's not as if you can turn it off and not take phone calls. It doesn't work like that.

And so it was time to get a break and that's why it happened at that time. There was no hidden agenda. I was just shot and needed a rest.

I couldn't go away thinking I would be coming back again

Once I had made my decision to leave Liverpool, if they had asked me to change my mind two months later I would have come back like a shot, but I couldn't go away thinking I was coming back.

Eventually I returned to football with Blackburn and we won the Premier League. It sounds easy doesn't it, but it never is. It was similar to the set-up at Liverpool at Ewood Park.

Blackburn had really good people at the football club. I had a fantastic coach in Ray Harford who was a huge influence and help. He was a great ally for me; good with the players and a very knowledgeable coach who could get his message over.

The club was in the second division when I started in the October. We finished sixth, got in the play-offs spots and won the final with a penalty against Leicester. That was us in the Premier League.

Alan Shearer came in and after that a lot of other players joined us on the back of that one signing.

Alan was a huge influence in Blackburn winning matches, but Jack Walker was the man who made everything happen. He had the financial clout and the desire. It wasn't a publicity stunt for him because he loved the town and wanted to put something back.

He developed the ground, spent money on new players, built the training ground and all for the love of Blackburn – the club and the town – because that's where he was from and where he was brought up.

It was a really enjoyable place to work. The success came with it.

MY TOON VISION
BY KENNY DALGLISH

Before you ask ..I won't walk out

TIMETABLE OF THE DAY

£1MILLION A YEAR FORTOON BECKONS

From back page

My time on the Tyne was short but sweet

I took the Newcastle United manager's job in 1997 and I soon found that the city was very similar to Glasgow and Liverpool. It was a fantastic football city with fantastically loyal supporters.

It was fortunate that the job came up because Kevin Keegan was sitting in fourth spot in the Premier League so it wasn't as if it was a relegation fight.

Kevin, in his wisdom, decided that it was no longer for him. He got up and went. It was a great opportunity for me. I always knew how passionate the fans were and so I decided to go and have a go at it.

I went up in the January and in the end we finished second ahead of Liverpool on goal difference.

They drew 1-1 at Sheffield Wednesday and we beat Forest 5-0 in the last game of the season at St James' Park to put us through to the Champions League knock-out qualifier.

We played Dinamo Zagreb in the qualifying game. We then had Barcelona, Dynamo Kiev and PSV Eindhoven in the group stage. Alan Shearer got himself injured pre-season and was not fit. We met Barcelona at Newcastle and beat them 3-2. It was an unbelievable night.

We also got to the FA Cup Final that year but my time there didn't last too long into the following season, no more than a couple of games.

Newcastle was a great place to go and work at a fantastic football club. My kids loved it up there and we've all still got friends from that part of the world. Although it wasn't a huge amount of time that I was on Tyneside, it was still enjoyable.

Parkhead revisited

In the summer of 1999 I got a phone call from Alan MacDonald who was the chief executive up at Celtic. He said he would like me to go back up the road and oversee the football side of things.

I liked the thought of setting something up, working with the players and seeing how it might work out.

John Barnes went up to Celtic with me as manager. It didn't turn out how everyone hoped it would, especially for John. It was his first go in management and I underestimated the job a wee bit when I should never have underestimated the size of Celtic Football Club. It's massive.

John was pretty good with his training. His principles and philosophy of how he thought about the game were similar to those of Celtic.

He did an awful lot of good things, but defeat to Inverness Cally in the cup was the end of it.

I took over from John and eventually Martin O'Neill came in. He wanted his own people so that was the end for me at Celtic, but we won the League Cup when I was up there so I never came back empty handed.

Celtic is a fantastically big football club but at that time Rangers were really strong as well. For us it wasn't that successful, but if somebody came and turned the clock back and asked if I would still agree to go to Celtic at that stage in my life I would say yes.

I often go back up to Scotland to see the old players and it's always good.

I will never forget that Celtic Football Club took me on when I was a youngster. They were fantastic to me and will always have a place in my heart.

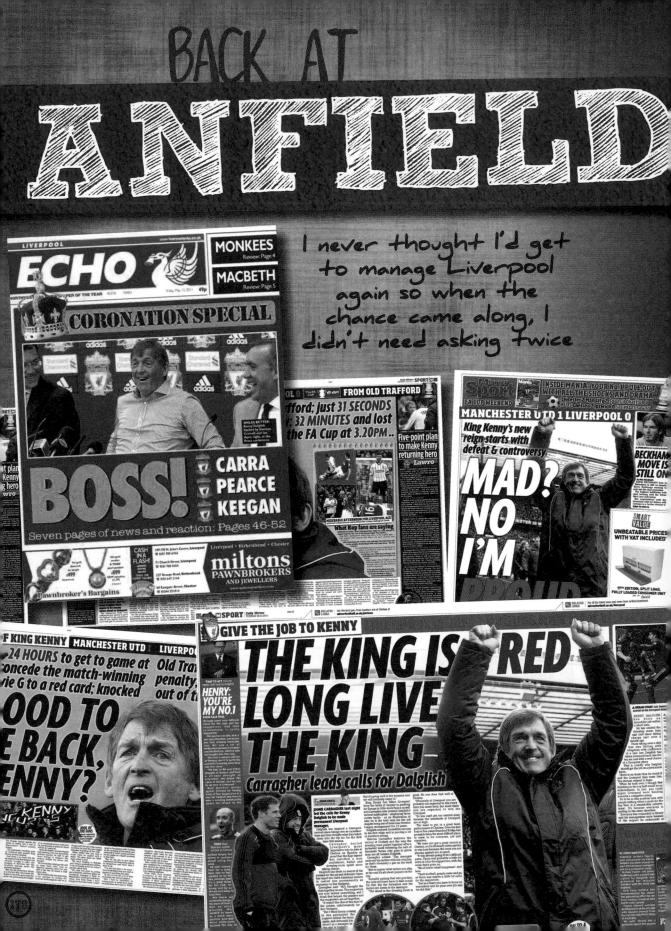

I never thought I'd get to manage Liverpool again so when the chance came along, I didn't need asking twice

In 2011 I got the call I thought would never come that would take me back to Anfield as Liverpool manager.

My first game was at Old Trafford in the FA Cup and the Liverpool fans gave me a wonderful welcome back.

The unfortunate thing for me was somebody got the sack for me to get the opportunity. I really admire Roy Hodgson and was sorry that it didn't work out the way everybody hoped it would.

When I was asked to return it was a no-brainer. I was back as Liverpool manager. I had left Liverpool in the middle of a season, so I went back to finish another one off!

Just to be back in amongst the people at Anfield meant a huge amount to me and my family.

We signed seven new players the following summer and for Liverpool Football Club to try and assimilate so many in one season was a huge ask for the players.

Liverpool Football Club is massive and the support it gets is fantastic. They had not won anything for six years when I got there, but we won something in our first season.

Some of those young lads at Liverpool are going to be really good footballers, but the club had never brought seven new players in before who would all start at the same time.

They would bring in one or two and allow them to get to know the club and their new surroundings.

What those boys achieved in 2012 was fantastic. To win the Carling Cup and to get to an FA Cup Final was beyond any expectations.

People will turn around and say we finished eighth in the league, but how many points would you swap for three Wembley trips? Because of the cup runs, it was probably a reason why the league results were not what we had hoped for, but the lads were fantastic and that can only stand them in good stead.

For Dirk Kuyt to have won his first medal at Liverpool Football Club after so long must have meant so much to him and to win a trophy at Wembley again clearly meant a lot to the fans. That League Cup was a trophy for Liverpool Football Club. I don't see that as anything but a positive.

It's always pleasant to get a winner's medal. Nowadays it's also a success to finish in the top four and get into the Champions League.

It might be more rewarding to qualify in Europe after finishing fourth, but who remembers that game when you finished fourth

OFFICIAL MATCHDAY PROGRAMME

CARLING CUP FINAL 2012

CARDIFF CITY FC · LIVERPOOL FC

26TH FEBRUARY 2012, 4.00PM KICK OFF
WEMBLEY STADIUM

£7.00

SPORT — Daily Mirror

CARLING CUP FINAL — CARDIFF CITY 2 — LIVERPOOL 2 — LIVERPOOL WIN 3-2 ON PENS

Rome..Cardiff.. Istanbul..Wembley was the most sensational of all

DRAMA OF THIS SHOOT-OUT PUTS OTHER GREAT KOP PENALTY VICTORIES IN SHADE

Wembley thrice

WEMBLEY TRIP 1: CARLING CUP FINAL
LIVERPOOL 2 CARDIFF 2 (LIVERPOOL WIN 3-2 ON PENALTIES)

ECHO
THE VOICE OF LIVERPOOL
WIN A SUPERMARKET DASH

MAN,
LONDO
MURDE
SHOCK

THIS IS JUST
HE START!

coverage in your souvenir

CARLING

CARDIFF
ERPOOL FC
1978
ALGLIS LIVERPOOL

39

T IS OVER SIX-YEAR TROPHY DROUGHT ENDS WITH CARLING CUP
GGER AND BETTER
r: It's great to
pean football
now we must
ampions League

We're going to

to get there? Winning a cup final against Cardiff at Wembley and walking away with the Carling Cup was a day to remember.

Yes, I would have loved to have finished fourth and I would have loved to have won the Champions League and won the Premier League, but it was never going to be achieved overnight.

If you take short steps you have got a chance and what we achieved was a positive move.

What was really pleasing was the response after the Carling Cup Final when we played Arsenal. We were magnificent at Anfield, but got beaten 2-1. Arsene Wenger said to me afterwards: "Kenny, I'm sorry. I don't know how we got anything from that game."

I could tell then that the quality of performance was coming. The boys' attitude and their commitment and desire to be successful was really becoming evident, which was also thanks to the hard work of Steve Clarke and Kevin Keen.

THE FA CUP WITH BUDWEISER
SEMI-FINAL 2012
12:30PM SATURDAY 14 APRIL, WEMBLEY STADIUM
OFFICIAL MATCHDAY PROGRAMME £5

LIVERPOOL v EVERTON

WEMBLEY TRIP 2: FA CUP SEMI-FINAL
LIVERPOOL 2 EVERTON 1

FA CUP SEMI-FINAL LIVERPOOL V EVERTON, WEMBLEY, KO 12.30PM

TEARS FOR FEARS

Carragher desperate to avoid Wembley agony he suffered as weeping Everton fan

GIBSON FLOWERS AFTER FINDING PLACE IN SUN

Wembley thrice

THE FA CUP WITH BUDWEISER

FINAL 2012

5:15PM SATURDAY 5 MAY 2012, WEMBLEY STADIUM
OFFICIAL MATCHDAY PROGRAMME £10

CHELSEA v LIVERPOOL

WEMBLEY TRIP 3: FA CUP FINAL
LIVERPOOL 1 CHELSEA 2

Special rapport with the fans

I have always had a good rapport with the Liverpool supporters. I have always tried my very best for Liverpool, as a player and a manager.

At the end of the day, we are fulfilling a dream for the supporters by playing for the club or managing the club. We've got to respect that. We've got to ensure that nobody ever takes their support for granted.

I never did as a player and I never did as a manager. If I've got a special place in the heart of the fans, well that's reciprocal.

One incident that stands out in my memory is when we beat Manchester United 3-1 at Anfield in March 2011 a few days after my 60th birthday. The fans started singing 'Happy Birthday To You' when we were 3-0 up. Fergie said: "I didn't know it was your birthday." I answered: "It isn't!"

For me, I have always been fantastically well received by Liverpool fans. The fact that the club still means so much to me and my family is because of the support we have had from the supporters.

Everybody in my family knows what we have received and we will forever be grateful for that support.

Having the respect of Liverpool people is very important to us. It's reflected in Marina's charity which has been a huge success because of the support of the people. They know that we are totally appreciative of what they have done for us.

Players need a break from the game

It still comes as something of a surprise to many football supporters when they discover that their favourite players have hobbies and interests away from the game.

I understand how people can begin to believe that we do nothing else but play, train, think and talk about our profession.

But if that was the case, we would go stale. Like every other working person, a professional footballer must have some form of relaxation.

Me, I am very much a home-bird. I enjoy family life, being involved with the development of my two children and planning our futures with my wife, Marina. I would hate to think that my two bairns, Kelly and Paul, had grown up without my realising it.

It also comes as a bit of a shock to fans when they discover that there are all sorts of reasons why a player is either off form or unavailable for reasons other than physical injury.

We do get colds, flu, stomach trouble, headaches etc. just like everyone else. Our domestic lives are no different either. Whether you work in a factory, shop or office, if your roof leaks, you have to call in a professional to do the repairs. If my roof leaks I have to call for the same assistance.

I believe very strongly in keeping my feet on the ground. Football is my living and my life. The fact that I love the game helps, but the fact remains that my career determines the welfare and security of my family.

In this respect I must aim to maintain as high a personal standard of play as humanly possible. Playing for Liverpool makes the task that much easier because I am playing in a great team, surrounded by some of the best professionals in the business.

But after working hard all week, training and preparing for a game, it does get to me. It is not so much pressure, more a realisation of what needs to be done. I like to get on with games and dislike waiting for the hours to tick by before the kick-off.

This makes for some pretty serious moods and it is Marina who has to put up with this side of the game. Just before a game I become totally wrapped up in it. Small, silly things can irritate me, things that I would normally never notice.

I find myself thinking a lot and saying very little. This leaves Marina to run the show and I have tremendous admiration for the way she, and the wives of so many professional footballers, handle this side of the life.

Do not misunderstand me. I am not talking about tempers, black moods or rows. But I for one know for a fact that I can become a bit tight inside and edgey as the game approaches.

Now imagine how this life would wear you down without a hobby or two away from the game.

Golf is one game I really enjoy. It is marvellous to pack my clubs into the back of the car and lose myself for a few hours around 18 holes.

Golf gives me a chance to get away from it all and unwind. I enjoy the fresh air, the relaxation and even the personal battle between that little white ball and me.

Inside my home I can spend endless hours with the kids, playing with them and getting to know them better every day. This, as any parent will agree, is a fascinating process in itself.

Yes, footballers are well-paid professional athletes and entertainers. But we are also fathers, husbands and guys who need a break from the game every now and again.

Champion and son...Kenny and Paul Dalglish celebrate the 1980 League Championship victory.

At home, away from the pressures of football. Kenny with his wife Marina, and children Kelly and Paul.

MY OTHER LIFE

Football has been my passion but I'd be nowhere without family, friends and fairways...

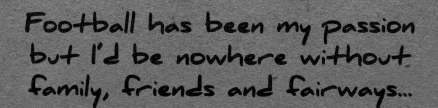

Page

Paul's the apple of ad's eye

'ALGLISH made a dream Scotland debut in
delighted dad, Kenny, at Airdrie last night
ung Newcastle

A great wife with a new life

I married Marina in 1974 and the great thing for me was that she settled very quickly when we left Glasgow for Liverpool.

It's easier for the lads. We can go to training in the morning with the other players and concentrate on the matches coming up. The women are left at home with the kids.

At first we stayed in Liverpool city centre at the old Holiday Inn in Paradise Street. The manager was a Scottish guy called Jack Ferguson who was a friend of Marina's dad.

It was like party time for us. Marina got friendly with all the staff and we settled quickly.

In fact, the girl who was the chambermaid, Cathy Murray, ended up being the babysitter and a friend for years. We felt comfortable in Liverpool and very happy with the environment and the generosity and the friendship of the people we were with.

Then we moved up the north coast of the Mersey to Southport where we have been ever since. In fact, we have been in England longer than we were in Scotland. It's home from home now.

We've moved houses a couple of times and while the kids would say they're Scottish, their roots are firmly in Southport.

Marina's charity keeps me busy

These days Marina has got her charity and she gave me my job back when I got the sack from Liverpool in 2012!

The Marina Dalglish Appeal was launched in 2005 to improve cancer care on Merseyside through various appeals. Marina has done brilliantly reacting the way she did to her own illness. The whole family gets involved in the fund-raising events.

Other than that, I still watch loads of football. I play golf. I do a wee bit of media and that's it.

I don't think it's particularly important to keep on top of my football knowledge. I just enjoy watching the matches.

You enjoy meeting the players and individuals and keeping up with the news within the game. Without being too dependent on it, you need something to have an interest in.

I'm not the only one in the family with an MBE. Marina was honoured by the Queen for her work for breast cancer patients

NEWCASTLE superkid Paul Dalglish... make... Under-... Estonia... Excels... Friday...

And... ing so... Army... Sheare... month... it at in...

The... recent... first-t...

boys for the next week.

"I didn't get a chance to play in our last game though I was...

"I'm feeling good at the moment after breaking into the first-team at Newcastle. However, I'm certainly... king any-... r granted. ...t to play...

the best England players ever and he's always offering me advice and passing on tips to bring my game on a little bit.

"He was happy that I was named in the Scotland squad and...

Pride in the kids and grandkids

Down the years, the kids have kept Marina busy rather than me. They are fantastic and we are very proud of all four of them. They have all done something in their own right, off their own back.

Kelly has developed a good career in the media.

Paul did really well in football and right now he is using that knowledge on the coaching side in America where he was voted Coach of the Year in the Premier Development League after leading Austin Aztex to the Championship.

Lynsey went to university and got a degree in sports management. She worked at the London Olympics and has a successful racehorse as well with a few other people.

Lauren helps Marina with the charity, but she got an honours degree in English as well which sounds strange – someone in my family doing that!

They have all found their own way in life and are happy, successful and healthy. And now they're contributing to the numbers in the Dalglish family themselves. Kelly has two daughters, Gabriella and Camilla, while Paul has twins called Rocco and Coco.

PAUL DALGLISH will make his debut for Scotland tonight under the watchful eye of his biggest footballing influence – his dad.

The Celtic, Liverpool and Scotland great, King Kenny will be in the stand at Airdrie's Excelsior stadium to see Paul line up in the Under 21 Euro match against...

career. He was a not a bad player really – average!"

That "average" player guided his son through the start of his career at Newcastle career before leaving the club earlier in the season.

Kenny said: "My... pretty...

definitely feel Scotti... accent doesn't matter t... 21 manager Alex Sm... reckons Dalglish des... opportunity.

He said: "No... at's just "No...

THE NEXT GENERATION:
My grandchildren Gabriella, Camilla, Rocco and Coco

COCO

ROCCO

CARLING

CARLING

not figured in new man-
ager Jimmy Quinn's plans
so far but has also been
nursing an ankle injury.
Hay said: "I have been
told that Aberdeen and St
Johnstone have both
made inquiries about me.

My life is a tale of two cities

Glasgow and Liverpool are both tough, working class cities, but if you know the area you live in, then you know what to expect.

My dad was a diesel engine fitter. My mum stayed at home, ran the house and did everything for my sister and me. We were just a normal Glasgow household.

Dad went to work all week, came in and gave my mum his wages. On a Saturday he got his pocket money back and went to the match with his mates.

If I played in the morning, he would always be there. Then we would go to the game, come back and have a wee kick-about in the garden while it was still light.

My dad would have his kippers, get a bit of a thirst up and go to the pub on a Saturday night. It was the normal way of life.

When I was a kid, it was no different to growing up in any industrial city. Glasgow has always been a great place, but it has developed into a real tourist centre these days.

Like Liverpool, it benefited from European Capital of Culture status. Over the last 10 years the development of both cities has been tremendous.

In a football sense, having been a Rangers fan and then having played for Celtic has not done me any harm. I don't think it matters really. It's not anybody's fault that you supported one team or represented the other.

I have never held any grudges against anybody. All you can do is go out and play for the team you are representing at that time.

My dad (pictured here with me) was a normal Glasgow man and he loved a plate of kippers

Liverpool and Glasgow links

The links between Glasgow and Liverpool are obvious. It meant that the move I made between the cities wasn't difficult.

The people are very similar. They have the same background with the ports and the shipyards. They have the same sense of humour. They have the same big city rivalry between their football teams.

The similarities are many and so it was easy for me to settle in Liverpool.

HAVING A ROUND

The golf bug

Anybody who can play an individual sport to the level some of the world class golfers play must be special.

Seve Ballesteros was fantastic. Everyone looked up to him because he was different.

I have to admire someone like Tiger Woods. He wins a tournament then makes sure he is back on the winning rostrum again. It will be interesting to see how he continues after his stumble.

Rory McIlroy is another great player. I just enjoy watching all of them.

When you see them play it's a different game entirely to the one we play. Their shots rise whereas ours just go up.

They are great to watch. You might get the same scores on the odd hole, but you don't get them the same way.

Pepe Reina in the water, Stevie Nicol left in a hole

It would be a close shave to name the best golfers amongst the former and current players on Merseyside. It would be between Kevin MacDonald, Gary Gillespie and big Hansen.

One that wasn't so good was Pepe Reina. Let's just say his ability didn't match his enthusiasm. He couldn't get across the water.

I suppose the most original golfer would be Stevie Nicol. He got his putting stroke banned because he used to stand facing the hole and putt side on!

Golf is not a serious game. It's good fun and it's good to see the players getting out there on the course.

Seve Ballesteros was a golfer to admire...

...Pepe Reina isn't

Stevie Nicol had his own style on the golf course

Loch Lomond golf course is my favourite

My favourite golf course

My favourite golf course is Loch Lomond because of everything that you get from the moment you go through the gates. Nobody can get near you. If you want some privacy you go there.

The course is immaculate. The views are stunning. I've never really played that much in America, but for me Loch Lomond is my favourite British course. I'm never any good, mind you, but I really enjoy it.

If you are a football amateur, it's almost impossible to play on famous grounds, but amateur golfers can play virtually anywhere in the world at the legendary venues, which is very unusual in sport.

It's changed a bit. A few people have played at Wembley on charity days and many have played at Anfield and Celtic Park, but they are not as lucky as the golfers.

'Alan Hansen, Graeme Souness and I have always been very close. Every time we won a trophy there was always a 'Jock' picture'

ANFIELD ACTION STATIONS . . . Alan Hansen, John Wark, Gary Gillespie, Dalglish, and Steve Nicol.

Noisy neighbours

Alan Hansen lives just around the corner from me.

I can't so much hear him shouting 'diabolical' at the telly when Match of the Day is on as 'fore' when he hits a wayward shot on the golf course!

He came to Liverpool in May 1977, I came in the August and Graeme Souness arrived the following January. We have always been very close, and every time we won a trophy there was always a 'Jock' picture.

It started off with us three and then Gary Gillespie came in. John Wark and Stevie Nicol followed, so we always made sure the rest of the lads knew we were the superior race!

Cheers

If ever I'm asked what my favourite drink is I normally say 'one that comes in a glass!' I don't drink beer or spirits. I'm a red or white wine drinker.

Just cook will yer!

Do I like my food? Lots of it! Can I cook? No! I'm hopeless.

It's amazing how times change. You used to come home as a kid and get your mince and potatoes, your ham, gammon and chicken. Now it's Italian, Chinese, Thai and Indian. I'm not a fussy eater. I'll have a go at anything and everything – and enjoy it.

At one of Marina's events, one of the prizes was for me to cook for 60 at a local restaurant. How did it go? I was there in body! Chef Simon Rimmer was doing all of the serious stuff.

I've acted as a chef two or three times, once being in a competition against Alan Stubbs, the ex-Everton and Celtic defender.

I've had a go at cooking but Simon Rimmer (below) did all the serious stuff

HAVING A LAUGH

My first car...and Alan Kennedy's Lada

Marina could actually drive before me, and she is younger. I never passed my driving test until I was about 20. Nowadays that's old. Marina used to pick me up.

The first car I got was a Fiat 124 because we knew a guy in the garage in Glasgow. I always wanted a Triumph Vitesse because I liked the style of the lights in the front. I don't know why, but that is what I always wanted.

I had a couple of World Cup cars like a Vauxhall VX 4/90, which was a wee bit too fast for me and I didn't know too much about what was under the bonnet.

The petrol heads will tell you that it had a twin-carburettor, high-compression, engine giving 71 bhp and servo-assisted brakes. Externally the car was distinguished from the standard model by one of those 'go faster' coloured stripes down the side, revised grille and larger tail-light clusters.

Don't be impressed. I just looked that up on Google! It was just a car to me.

I've had a few cars, but all they have to do is get me from A to B with the golf clubs in the boot and I'm happy.

Lada had sponsorship deals with Everton, Liverpool and Bolton when I was at Anfield.

Three of the lads at Liverpool used to get Ladas and Alan Kennedy was one of them. He used to park his car in town. He could even take his gear stick out and walk away!

Someone broke into the vehicle once – they left the car but took his coat!

Fiat 124

Some cars similar to the ones I had (or wanted) in my younger days

Triumph Vitesse

Vauxhall VX 4/90

Same stories, same punch lines, but we still laugh at every one

I still meet up with some of the old Liverpool lads from time to time. Phil Thompson organises a get-together at Christmas. Sometimes there's a mid-season gathering arranged with the help of Sammy Lee.

It's great to see the lads. Every year it's the same stories. Every year we laugh at the same punchlines. It's unbelievable, but it's all about just getting together.

These days a lot of the former players work at the ground on match days and that is great. People can see faces they recognise from the pitch.

There are five or six of us who see more of each other. Alan Hansen, Mark Lawrenson, Jim Beglin, Ronnie Whelan, Gary Gillespie. If I've forgotten anybody then it's only my age.

Stevie Mac used to live near to us as well. It's great to keep in touch.

A picture of me, Sandy Jardine and our wives in the 1970s, but Sandy and me didn't get to number one, unlike the Hillsborough Justice song that topped the charts in 2012

Singing with Sandy

During my Celtic days I was persuaded to record a single with my Scotland team-mate Sandy Jardine. Somebody was the lead singer on that song, but I couldn't say it was me!

It didn't reach the charts and let's just say we were not called back into the studio to make a follow-up. I'm definitely not a karaoke king. I'm much better at miming.

By the way, I should add that I did have a Christmas number one hit with the Liverpool boys.

We recorded the old Hollies song 'He Ain't Heavy, He's My Brother' to raise funds for the Hillsborough Justice Campaign at the end of 2012 and we were all delighted when it topped the charts at Christmas.

It raised money for an important cause although I think it's safe to say it'll go down as my only number one Christmas hit!

What do you think, Kenny? Oh Yeah!

My other brush with the charts came before the 1988 FA Cup final when we recorded The Anfield Rap. It got to number three in the charts but I'm not sure any of us would've made it onto X-Factor! I know two who wouldn't have impressed Simon Cowell...Hansen and Dalglish!

It was a good record, a good bit of patter amongst the lads and a mixture of cultures. I think they only asked me to get involved so they could all get some time off!

The King's honours list

Liverpool
(as player, player-manager or manager)

European Cup: 1978, 1981, 1984

League championship: 1978–79, 1979–80, 1981–82, 1982–83, 1983–84, 1985–86, 1987-88, 1989-90

FA Cup: 1986, 1989

League Cup: 1981, 1982, 1983, 1984, 2012

Charity Shield: 1977, 1979, 1980, 1982, 1986, 1988, 1989, 1990

UEFA Super Cup: 1977

Celtic
(as player or manager)

League championship: 1971-72, 1972-73, 1973-74, 1976-77

Scottish Cup: 1972, 1974, 1975, 1977

Scottish League Cup: 1975, 2000

Blackburn
(as manager)

League championship: 1994-95

Scotland

Most caps for Scotland (102)
Most goals for Scotland (30)

Individual honours

Ballon d'Or Silver Award: 1983

FWA Footballer of the Year: 1979, 1983

PFA Player of the Year: 1983

FWA Tribute Award: 1987

Scottish Premier Division Golden Boot: 1976

Manager of the Year Award: 1986, 1988, 1990, 1995

Freedom of the City of Glasgow: 1986

Inaugural Inductee to the English Football Hall of Fame: 2002

Member of the Scotland Football Hall of Fame: 2004

MBE: 1985

King Kenny's top Kop tunes

Every Other Saturday

Every other Saturday's me half day off
And it's off to the match I go
I like to take a stroll along the Anfield Road
Me and me old pal Joe
I like to see the lasses with their red scarves on
I like to hear the Kopites roar
But I don't have to tell you that best of all
Is when we see Liverpool sc-o-o-o-ore

We've won the English league about a thousand times
And Uefa was a simple do
We've played some exhibitions in the FA Cup
We are the Wembley Wizards too
But when we won the European Cup in Rome
Like we should have done years before
We gathered down at Anfield
Boys a hundred thousand strong
To give the boys a welcome ho-om-me

Kenny ohhh Kenny
I'd walk a million miles for one of your goals oh Kenny
ohhh Kenny

Dalglish!

(clap, clap, clap-clap-clap,
clap-clap-clap-clap)
Dalglish!

Fields of Anfield Road

All round the Fields of Anfield Road
Where once we watched the King Kenny play (and could he play)
Stevie Heighway on the wing
We had dreams and songs to sing
Of the glory round the Fields of Anfield Road

A Liverbird upon my Chest

Here's a song about a football team
The greatest team you've ever seen
A team that play total football
They've won the league, Europe and all

Chorus: A Liverbird upon my chest
We are the men, of Shankly's best
A team that plays the Liverpool way
And wins the Championship in May

With Kenny Dalglish on the ball
He was the greatest of them all
And Ian Rush, four goals or two
Left Evertonians feeling blue
Chorus
Now if you go down Goodison Way
Hard luck stories you hear each day
There's not a trophy to be seen
'Cos Liverpool have swept them clean
Chorus
Now on the glorious 10th of May
There's laughing reds on Wembley Way
We're full of smiles and joy and glee
It's Everton 1 and Liverpool 3
Chorus

Now on the 20th of May
We're laughing still on Wembley Way
Those Evertonians feeling blue
at Liverpool 3 and Everton 2
Chorus
And as we sang round Goodison Park
With crying blues all in a nark
They're probably crying still
at Liverpool 5 and Everton 0
Chorus
We remember them with pride
Those mighty Reds of Shankly's side
And Kenny's boys of '88
There's never been a side so great
Chorus
Now back in 1965
When great Bill Shankly was alive
We're playing Leeds, the score's 1-1
When it fell to the head of Ian St John
Chorus
On April 15th '89
What should have been a joyous time
Ninety-six friends, we all shall miss
And all the Kopites want justice

My career timeline

August 1971
Netted from the penalty spot in a 2-0 League Cup win against Rangers at Ibrox to open goalscoring account for Celtic

September 1971
Scored first league goal in a green and white shirt in the 9-1 thrashing of Clyde at Celtic Park

October 1971
Struck first career hat-trick as Dundee were defeated 3-1 at Parkhead

1968　1969　1971

April 1968
Signed full professional terms for Celtic Football Club at the age of 17

September 1968
Made senior Celtic debut as a substitute for Charlie Gallagher in a 4-2 Scottish League Cup quarter-final victory at Hamilton Academical

October 1969
Handed first league start for the Bhoys in a 7-1 win against Raith Rovers at Parkhead

October 1971
Found the net in the Scottish League Cup final but ended up on the losing side to Partick Thistle who ran out 4-1 winners

November 1971
Received first full international cap for Scotland at the age of 20 when brought on as a substitute against Belgium at Pittodrie

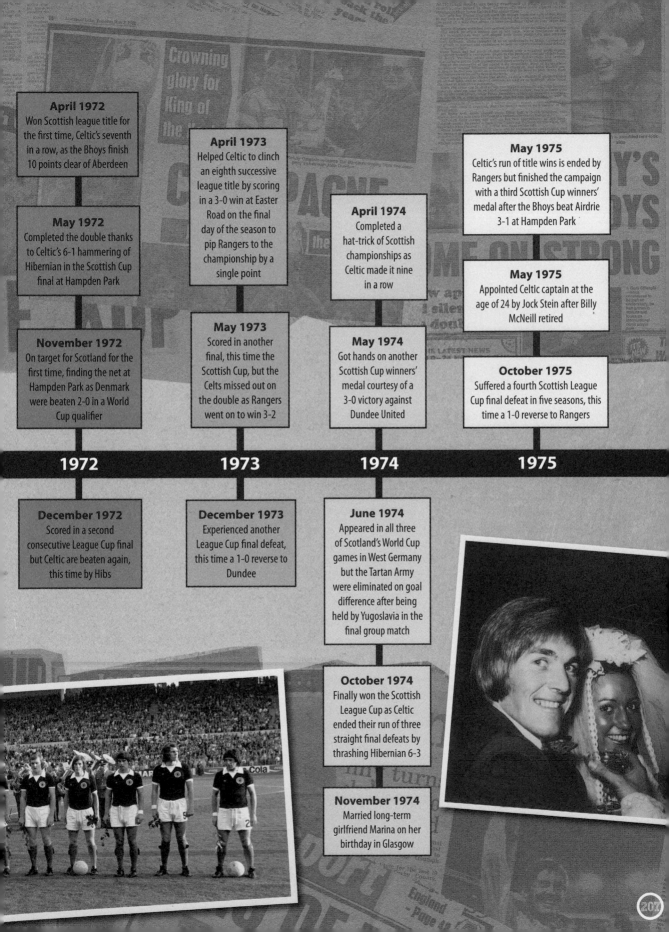

April 1972
Won Scottish league title for the first time, Celtic's seventh in a row, as the Bhoys finish 10 points clear of Aberdeen

May 1972
Completed the double thanks to Celtic's 6-1 hammering of Hibernian in the Scottish Cup final at Hampden Park

November 1972
On target for Scotland for the first time, finding the net at Hampden Park as Denmark were beaten 2-0 in a World Cup qualifier

April 1973
Helped Celtic to clinch an eighth successive league title by scoring in a 3-0 win at Easter Road on the final day of the season to pip Rangers to the championship by a single point

May 1973
Scored in another final, this time the Scottish Cup, but the Celts missed out on the double as Rangers went on to win 3-2

April 1974
Completed a hat-trick of Scottish championships as Celtic made it nine in a row

May 1974
Got hands on another Scottish Cup winners' medal courtesy of a 3-0 victory against Dundee United

May 1975
Celtic's run of title wins is ended by Rangers but finished the campaign with a third Scottish Cup winners' medal after the Bhoys beat Airdrie 3-1 at Hampden Park

May 1975
Appointed Celtic captain at the age of 24 by Jock Stein after Billy McNeill retired

October 1975
Suffered a fourth Scottish League Cup final defeat in five seasons, this time a 1-0 reverse to Rangers

1972   **1973**   **1974**   **1975**

December 1972
Scored in a second consecutive League Cup final but Celtic are beaten again, this time by Hibs

December 1973
Experienced another League Cup final defeat, this time a 1-0 reverse to Dundee

June 1974
Appeared in all three of Scotland's World Cup games in West Germany but the Tartan Army were eliminated on goal difference after being held by Yugoslavia in the final group match

October 1974
Finally won the Scottish League Cup as Celtic ended their run of three straight final defeats by thrashing Hibernian 6-3

November 1974
Married long-term girlfriend Marina on her birthday in Glasgow

My career timeline

April 1976
Ended the inaugural season of the Scottish Premier League without silverware for the first time as Rangers pip Celtic to top spot, but 24 league goals earn the Golden Boot

April 1977
Skippered Celtic to the title as they completed the campaign unbeaten at Parkhead

May 1979
Scored 21st league goal of the season, (best tally in a Liverpool shirt) as the Reds beat Aston Villa 3-0 to clinch the league title

May 1977
Lifted the Scottish Cup at Hampden Park as the Bhoys clinch the double with a 1-0 success in an Old Firm final

January 1978
Struck first hat-trick for Liverpool in a 3-1 League Cup win at Wrexham

May 1976
Scored the winner in front of over 85,000 at Hampden Park as Scotland beat England 2-1 to win the home championship outright for the first time since 1967

June 1977
Produced a Wembley winner against England as Scotland retain the home championship to spark one of the most famous pitch invasions of all time

March 1978
Experienced another League Cup final defeat, this time at Old Trafford as Liverpool lost a replay 1-0 to Nottingham Forest

May 1979
Awarded the Football Writers' Footballer of the Year Award in recognition of an outstanding season in a red shirt

1976   1977   1978   1979

October 1976
Reached a century of league goals for Celtic in a 2-0 win against Motherwell

August 1977
Ended Celtic career by signing for European champions Liverpool for a club record transfer fee of £440,000

May 1978
Ended first season in England in glorious fashion by scoring the winning goal in the European Cup final against Bruges at Wembley as Bob Paisley's men retained the trophy

August 1979
On target at Wembley again as Liverpool opened the season by beating Arsenal 3-1 in the Charity Shield

November 1976
Scored Celtic's goal in the Scottish League Cup final against Aberdeen but the Dons ran out 2-1 winners

August 1977
Made Reds debut in a 0-0 draw against Manchester United in the Charity Shield at Wembley before marking league debut at Middlesbrough with a goal

October 1977
Marked 50th cap for Scotland with a goal against Wales at Anfield to secure qualification for the 1978 World Cup in Argentina

June 1978
Broke Denis Law's 55-cap appearance record in the World Cup finals and scored in a famous 3-2 victory against Holland but Scotland were eliminated at the group stage

December 1977
Scored in Liverpool's 6-0 European Super Cup final second leg win against Kevin Keegan's SV Hamburg at Anfield to win my first European medal with the Reds

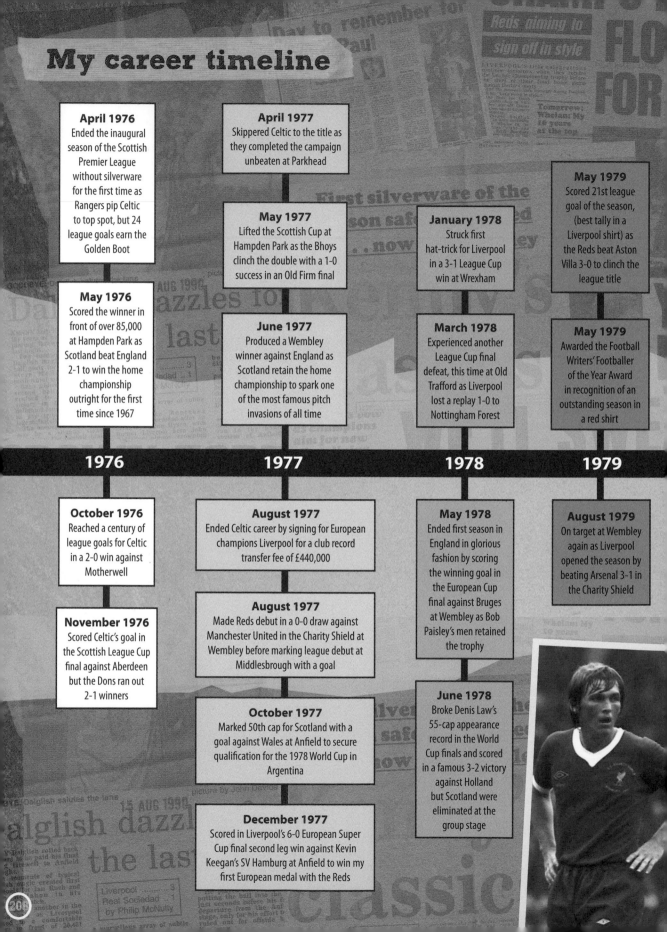

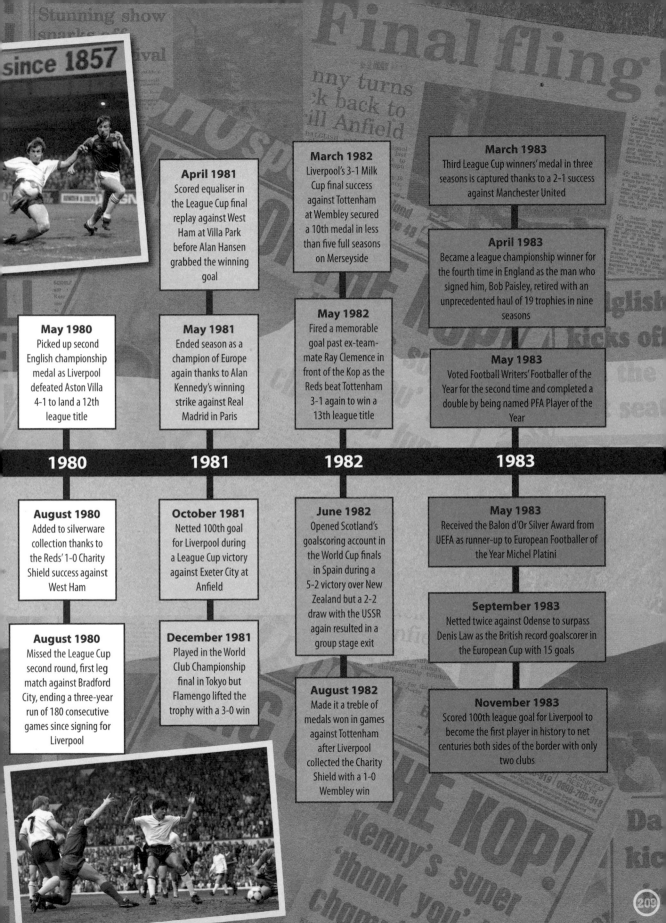

April 1981
Scored equaliser in the League Cup final replay against West Ham at Villa Park before Alan Hansen grabbed the winning goal

March 1982
Liverpool's 3-1 Milk Cup final success against Tottenham at Wembley secured a 10th medal in less than five full seasons on Merseyside

March 1983
Third League Cup winners' medal in three seasons is captured thanks to a 2-1 success against Manchester United

April 1983
Became a league championship winner for the fourth time in England as the man who signed him, Bob Paisley, retired with an unprecedented haul of 19 trophies in nine seasons

May 1980
Picked up second English championship medal as Liverpool defeated Aston Villa 4-1 to land a 12th league title

May 1981
Ended season as a champion of Europe again thanks to Alan Kennedy's winning strike against Real Madrid in Paris

May 1982
Fired a memorable goal past ex-team-mate Ray Clemence in front of the Kop as the Reds beat Tottenham 3-1 again to win a 13th league title

May 1983
Voted Football Writers' Footballer of the Year for the second time and completed a double by being named PFA Player of the Year

1980   1981   1982   1983

August 1980
Added to silverware collection thanks to the Reds' 1-0 Charity Shield success against West Ham

October 1981
Netted 100th goal for Liverpool during a League Cup victory against Exeter City at Anfield

June 1982
Opened Scotland's goalscoring account in the World Cup finals in Spain during a 5-2 victory over New Zealand but a 2-2 draw with the USSR again resulted in a group stage exit

May 1983
Received the Balon d'Or Silver Award from UEFA as runner-up to European Footballer of the Year Michel Platini

August 1980
Missed the League Cup second round, first leg match against Bradford City, ending a three-year run of 180 consecutive games since signing for Liverpool

December 1981
Played in the World Club Championship final in Tokyo but Flamengo lifted the trophy with a 3-0 win

September 1983
Netted twice against Odense to surpass Denis Law as the British record goalscorer in the European Cup with 15 goals

August 1982
Made it a treble of medals won in games against Tottenham after Liverpool collected the Charity Shield with a 1-0 Wembley win

November 1983
Scored 100th league goal for Liverpool to become the first player in history to net centuries both sides of the border with only two clubs

209

My career timeline

March 1986
Made a Freeman of Glasgow by the Lord Provost in a ceremony in native city

March 1984
Returned from two months out injured with a fractured cheekbone to help Liverpool land fourth consecutive League Cup by beating Everton 1-0 in a replay at Maine Road

February 1985
Visited Buckingham Palace with family to receive MBE for services to football the day before 750th club career appearance

March 1986
Received solid silver cap from Franz Beckenbauer and made captain for the night to mark 100th appearance for Scotland, a 3-0 win against Romania at Hampden Park

April 1987
Took the Reds to the Littlewoods Cup final against Arsenal but lost 2-1, the first time Liverpool had ever been beaten when Ian Rush scored

May 1984
Won another league championship medal, this time under the management of Joe Fagan, as Liverpool became the first post-war side to win three consecutive titles

May 1985
Played in European Cup final but Juventus' 1-0 win is overshadowed by the deaths of 39 of their supporters following crowd trouble before the game at Heysel

May 1986
Scored the goal that won Liverpool the league title at Chelsea on a dramatic final day of the season

April 1987
Scored 172nd and final goal in a Liverpool shirt during a 3-0 victory against Nottingham Forest at Anfield

May 1986
Became the first Reds boss to lead the club to a league and FA Cup double when Liverpool beat Everton 3-1 at Wembley in the first all-Merseyside FA Cup final

1984   1985   1986   1987

May 1984
Celebrated third European Cup medal as Liverpool defeated AS Roma on penalties in their own stadium to complete first English treble of trophies in the same season

May 1985
Appointed player-manager of Liverpool Football Club at the age of 34 following Joe Fagan's retirement

May 1986
Named as Football League Manager of the Year in recognition of a remarkable first season at Anfield as Liverpool player-manager

July 1987
Signed Peter Beardsley for club record £1.9m, having previously bought John Aldridge and John Barnes

November 1984
Sent off for the only time in entire career for retaliation during Liverpool's European Cup second round clash with Benfica in Estadio da Luz

September 1985
Made Aston Villa midfielder Steve McMahon first signing as a manager in a £350,000 deal

June 1986
Missed out on becoming the first Brit to play in four World Cups when knee injury forced withdrawal from the Scotland squad bound for Mexico

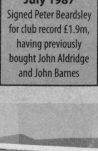

November 1984
Found the net for Scotland in a 3-1 victory over Spain at Hampden Park to equal Denis Law's record of 30 goals at international level

August 1985
Won first game as Liverpool manager 2-0 against Arsenal through goals from Ronnie Whelan and Steve Nicol

September 1986
Led Liverpool to a 7-2 aggregate success in the Screen Sport Super Cup final against Everton

November 1986
Received record 102nd and final cap for Scotland in a 3-0 victory over Luxembourg at Hampden Park

March 1988
Reds equalled Leeds United's record of going 29 Division One games unbeaten from the start of the season but were beaten in the 30th match, 1-0 at Goodison Park

April 1989
Experienced the worst day of career as the Reds' FA Cup semi-final against Nottingham Forest at Hillsborough was abandoned when crushing in the Leppings Lane end resulted in the deaths of 96 Liverpool supporters

April 1990
Led Liverpool to a record 18th league title with two games to spare courtesy of a 2-1 victory against QPR

April 1988
Watched Liverpool storm to a 17th league title playing football dubbed 'better than the Brazilians' culminating in famous 5-0 win against Brian Clough's Nottingham Forest

April 1989
Took team up to Celtic Park and scored in a Disaster Appeal game, the club's first since Hillsborough, which raised over £300,000 for the families

May 1990
Came on for 19 minutes at home to Derby County to make 515th and final appearance of Liverpool playing career at the age of 39

1988   1989   1990

May 1988
Saw team fail to complete second double in three years when Wimbledon shocked the Reds 1-0 in FA Cup final at Wembley

May 1989
Led Liverpool to victory in the FA Cup final with a 3-2 win against Everton after beating Forest 3-1 in a rearranged semi-final at Old Trafford

May 1990
Named as Football League Manager of the Year for the third time following Liverpool's title success

May 1988
Received Football League Manager of the Year award for the second time

May 1989
Missed out on another double when Michael Thomas scored a last minute goal at Anfield in the final match of the campaign to give Arsenal a dramatic championship win

August 1990
Played for 75 minutes in Anfield testimonial against Real Sociedad in front of a crowd of 30,461

August 1988
Won first Charity Shield as manager thanks to Liverpool's 2-1 victory against Wimbledon

August 1989
Began fifth season as Liverpool boss with 1-0 Charity Shield win against the Gunners at Wembley

My career timeline

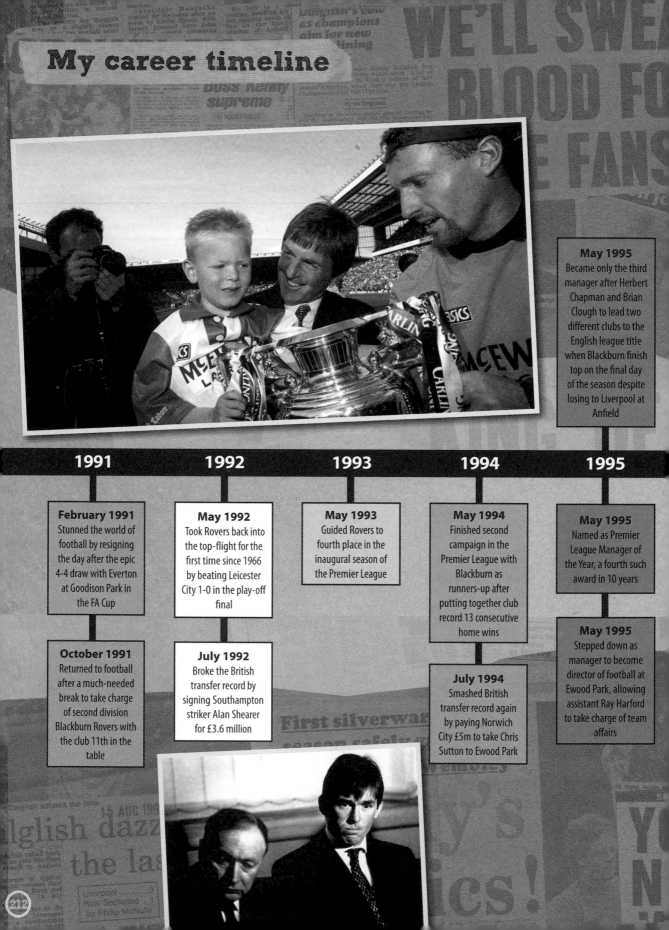

May 1995
Became only the third manager after Herbert Chapman and Brian Clough to lead two different clubs to the English league title when Blackburn finish top on the final day of the season despite losing to Liverpool at Anfield

1991 **1992** **1993** **1994** **1995**

February 1991
Stunned the world of football by resigning the day after the epic 4-4 draw with Everton at Goodison Park in the FA Cup

May 1992
Took Rovers back into the top-flight for the first time since 1966 by beating Leicester City 1-0 in the play-off final

May 1993
Guided Rovers to fourth place in the inaugural season of the Premier League

May 1994
Finished second campaign in the Premier League with Blackburn as runners-up after putting together club record 13 consecutive home wins

May 1995
Named as Premier League Manager of the Year, a fourth such award in 10 years

October 1991
Returned to football after a much-needed break to take charge of second division Blackburn Rovers with the club 11th in the table

July 1992
Broke the British transfer record by signing Southampton striker Alan Shearer for £3.6 million

July 1994
Smashed British transfer record again by paying Norwich City £5m to take Chris Sutton to Ewood Park

May 1995
Stepped down as manager to become director of football at Ewood Park, allowing assistant Ray Harford to take charge of team affairs

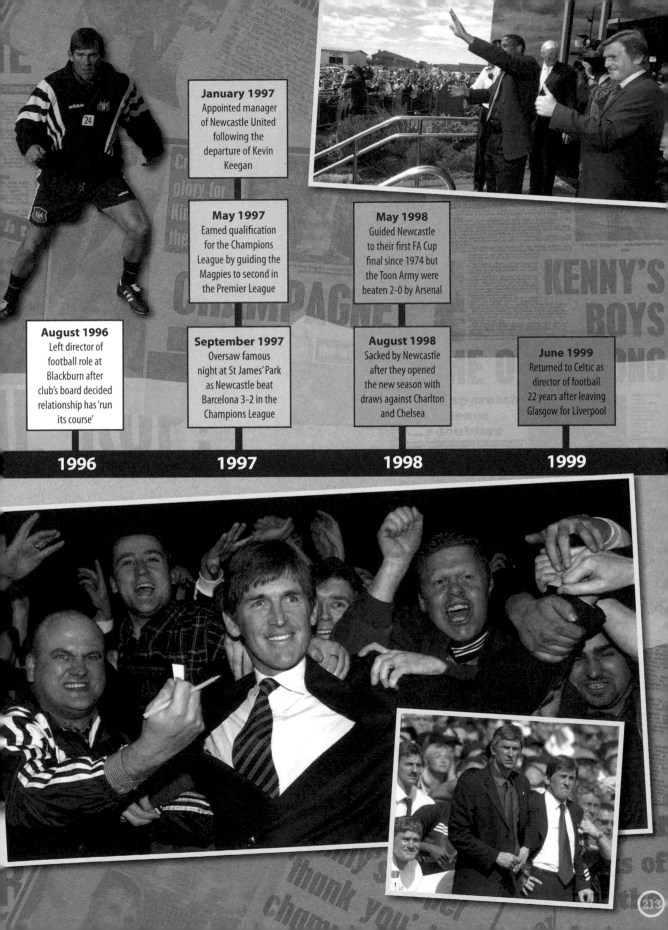

January 1997
Appointed manager of Newcastle United following the departure of Kevin Keegan

May 1997
Earned qualification for the Champions League by guiding the Magpies to second in the Premier League

May 1998
Guided Newcastle to their first FA Cup final since 1974 but the Toon Army were beaten 2-0 by Arsenal

August 1996
Left director of football role at Blackburn after club's board decided relationship has 'run its course'

September 1997
Oversaw famous night at St James' Park as Newcastle beat Barcelona 3-2 in the Champions League

August 1998
Sacked by Newcastle after they opened the new season with draws against Charlton and Chelsea

June 1999
Returned to Celtic as director of football 22 years after leaving Glasgow for Liverpool

1996   **1997**   **1998**   **1999**

My career timeline

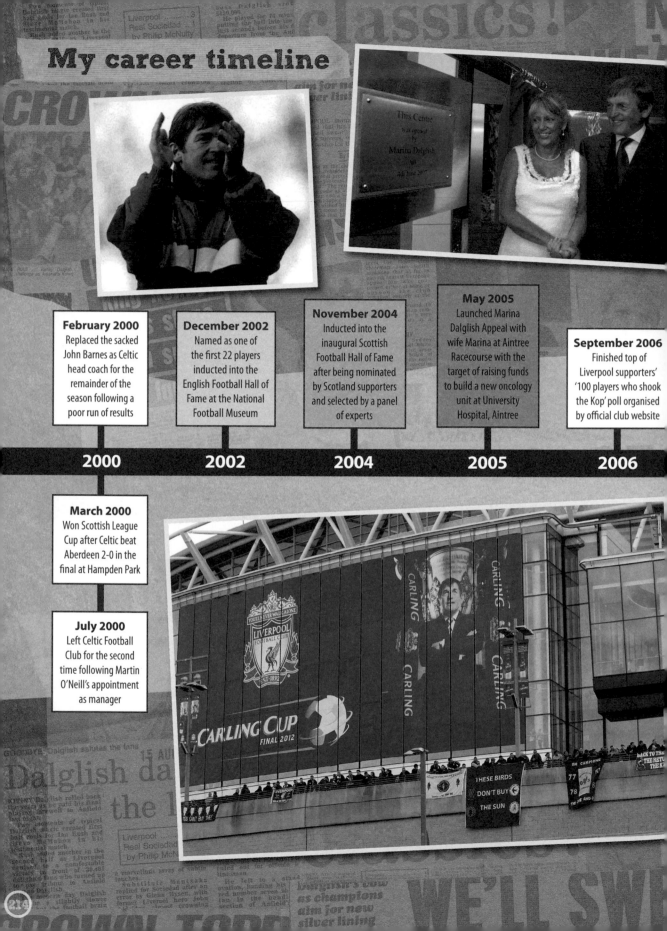

February 2000
Replaced the sacked John Barnes as Celtic head coach for the remainder of the season following a poor run of results

December 2002
Named as one of the first 22 players inducted into the English Football Hall of Fame at the National Football Museum

November 2004
Inducted into the inaugural Scottish Football Hall of Fame after being nominated by Scotland supporters and selected by a panel of experts

May 2005
Launched Marina Dalglish Appeal with wife Marina at Aintree Racecourse with the target of raising funds to build a new oncology unit at University Hospital, Aintree

September 2006
Finished top of Liverpool supporters' '100 players who shook the Kop' poll organised by official club website

2000 **2002** **2004** **2005** **2006**

March 2000
Won Scottish League Cup after Celtic beat Aberdeen 2-0 in the final at Hampden Park

July 2000
Left Celtic Football Club for the second time following Martin O'Neill's appointment as manager

January 2011
Made an emotional return to the Liverpool manager's job after almost 20 years when asked to take over until the end of the season following the departure of Roy Hodgson

February 2012
Led the Reds to first piece of silverware since 2006 by beating Cardiff City on penalties in Carling Cup final at Wembley

July 2009
Returned to Liverpool as club ambassador after Rafa Benitez requested the appointment

May 2011
Named as Liverpool manager on a permanent basis following a successful five-month caretaker spell

May 2012
Narrowly failed to complete a cup double as Liverpool were beaten 2-1 by Chelsea in the FA Cup final

2009   2011   2012

May 2012
Sacked by Liverpool owners Fenway Sports Group

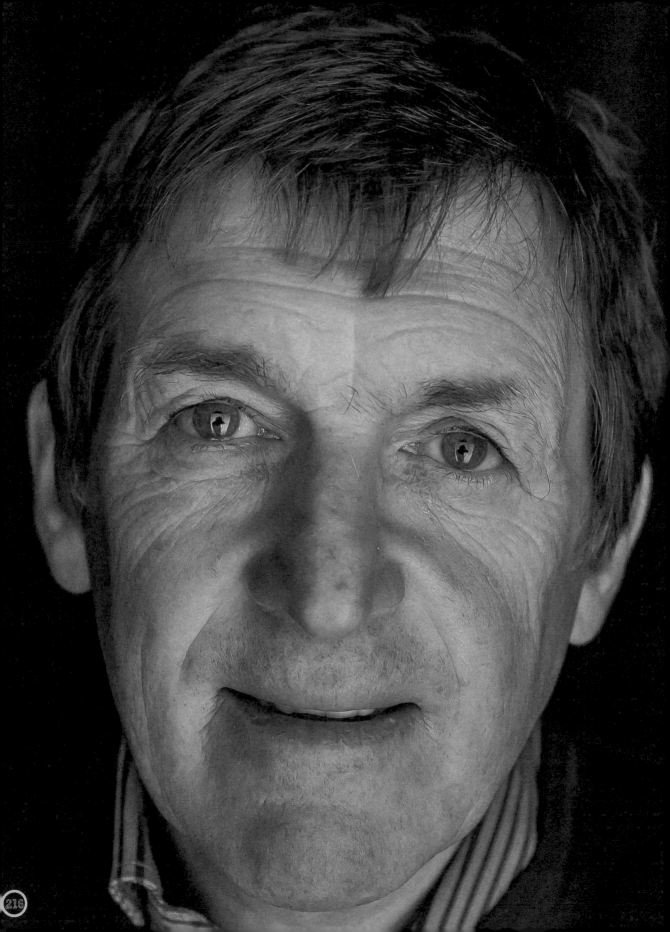

It's been a privilege

f I'd done this book five years ago I'd never have predicted that I would have returned to Anfield as Liverpool manager for a second time, so who knows what the future holds for me next?

I've always said that I am happy to help Liverpool Football Club in whatever way I can and that hasn't changed in any way, shape or form.

Having the respect of the Liverpool people is important to us as a family. We appreciate all the support we have received since coming down the road in 1977 and that is why the club and the city still mean so much to us now. I'm from Glasgow, and love going back up there, but Merseyside is now my home.

If anybody is thinking of offering me a job, though, they'll need to have a word with Marina first – she's taken me back on with her charity and as far as I know she's not planning to give me the sack!

I'm still involved in football through my Daily Mirror column and I'll always enjoy watching matches. Having a bit of extra time to spend on the golf course is also helpful as it means I can help Hansen search for his ball off the tee!

In all seriousness, I'd like to thank you all for buying my book. Putting it together has revived some wonderful memories for me, Marina and the kids and reminded me how privileged I have been to be involved with some of the greatest clubs in football.

Your support will always be appreciated by the Dalglish family.

GO INTERACTIVE WITH THE KING!

Download the Kenny Dalglish Digital ScrAppbook to see a hero come to life

You've read the book, now look out for the brand new app.

The **Kenny Dalglish Digital ScrAppbook** is an exciting new creation that allows you to get even closer to one of football's greatest legends and his collection of memorabilia.

Just like one of your dusty old scrapbooks it's packed with pictures, cuttings and memories, brought to you in an interactive format for the iPad and Android tablet.

The **Kenny Dalglish Digital ScrAppbook** features personal video and audio of the Liverpool and Celtic great talking you through his favourite belongings.

Packed with exclusives, it also allows you the experience of touching the medals to bring the stories behind them to life.

Hearing Kenny stories is always great, but having them told to you by the man himself takes the experience to a new level.

LOOK OUT FOR The Kenny Dalglish Digital ScrAppbook

THE PERFECT DOUBLE ACT

They looked great on the pitch together – now Rush and Dalglish can form the perfect partnership on your bookshelf

HIS AWARDS

HIS SHIRTS

HIS MEMORIES

One of the world's greatest goalscorers exclusively takes you through his huge array of personal treasures and his career in this superb hardback book

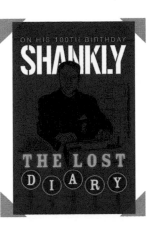
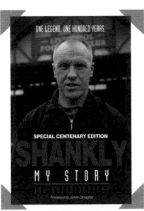
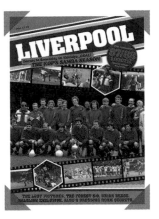

MY LIFE

Sport Media
A Trinity Mirror Business